LUKE EXPLAINED

LUKE EXPLAINED

Understanding the Book and Its Message for Today

Samuel Whitaker

Part of the Bible for Modern Life Series

Ascent Press

Scripture quotations taken from the Holy Bible, **New International Version® NIV®**
Copyright © 1973, 1978, 1984, 2011 by Biblica, Inc.
Used by permission. All rights reserved worldwide.

Published by
Ascent Press

ISBN: 978-1-972885-02-4

Printed in the United States of America

First Edition 2026

For those seeking clarity in the ancient words of Scripture.

CONTENTS

Disclaimer

This book provides an interpretive overview of the biblical text using historical scholarship and modern analysis tools. It is intended to help readers understand the themes, context, and message of the biblical narrative and is not intended to replace personal study of Scripture

Introduction

Why Luke Still Matters

Of the four Gospels, Luke is the one that will not let you forget who is missing from the room. Where Mark moves with relentless urgency, and Matthew builds a case from the inside of Jewish tradition, Luke keeps turning toward the edges — toward women, toward the poor, toward Samaritans and Gentiles, toward the people who have been told, in ways both formal and informal, that the story being told is not about them. It is about them. Luke insists on this with a gentleness that is itself a form of argument, a literary patience that allows the case to build across twenty-four chapters until there is no longer any reasonable ground for excluding anyone from the scope of what God has done.

Luke's Gospel is the longest of the four and the most deliberately composed. Its author announces this directly in the opening verses — a careful prologue addressed to a named recipient, written in the most polished Greek in the New Testament, describing a process of research, consultation of sources, and ordered arrangement designed to produce certainty in the reader. No other Gospel begins this way. No other Evangelist steps into view before the narrative begins to explain what he is doing and why. The prologue is brief, but its existence signals something essential about what follows: this is a Gospel that understands itself as literature, that takes the craft of narrative seriously, and that trusts the carefully ordered account to do theological work that argument alone cannot accomplish.

For readers who come to Luke expecting what they have found in Mark or Matthew, the experience has a different texture. The urgency of Mark is present but modulated — Luke moves at the pace of a writer who knows where the story is going and is confident it will get there. The Jewish argument of Matthew is present but expanded — Luke is equally interested in what the arrival of Jesus means for people who never read the prophets and never attended a synagogue. The Jesus of Luke prays more than any other Gospel's Jesus. He weeps over Jerusalem. He speaks to women in public with a directness that shocked his contemporaries. He eats with people whose company religious society regarded as contaminating. He tells stories that have no parallel in the rest of Scripture — stories whose power to disturb and console has not diminished across twenty centuries of reading.

That breadth is the entry point this book attempts to open. Reading Luke well requires more than familiarity with its most beloved passages. It requires understanding the world that shaped it, the sources its author drew upon, the structure that carries its theological argument, the themes that recur from the temple in Jerusalem to the road to Emmaus, and the specific portrait of Jesus that emerges when those themes are followed with the sustained attention they deserve. The chapters that follow provide that orientation — not as a substitute for reading the Gospel itself but as a map that allows the reader to navigate it with the understanding it is designed to produce.

Luke was not written in isolation, and it was not written for a narrow audience. The same author who composed this Gospel went on to write the Acts of the Apostles, and the two volumes together constitute the longest single contribution to the New Testament by any writer. The scope of the project — tracing the movement of the gospel from a stable in Bethlehem to the capital of the Roman Empire — is itself a theological statement about the range of what God intends. Luke's Jesus does not stay in Galilee. He does not stay in Israel. The story that begins with a birth announcement delivered to a peasant girl in a backwater province does not end until it has reached Rome, and the Gospel lays the foundation for that reach in every chapter.

The communities for whom Luke wrote were navigating questions that the other Gospels address only partially: What does the gospel mean for people who are not Jewish? What does it say to those who have been excluded not by ethnicity but by poverty, by gender, by the specific forms of social shame that first-century Mediterranean culture enforced with particular severity? What does faithful discipleship look like in a world where the expected return of the Lord has not yet occurred, and life must be lived with patience rather than imminence? These questions have not disappeared. They are the questions of every generation that has encountered the gospel in circumstances it was not originally addressed to and discovered, with surprise, that it speaks there with unusual clarity and unusual force.

Chapter 1

The Human Question

"Since I myself have carefully investigated everything from the beginning, I too decided to write an orderly account for you, most excellent Theophilus, so that you may know the certainty of the things you have been taught."
— Luke 1:3-4 (NIV)

The Universal Search for Certainty

Every serious human life eventually confronts the question of what can be known and what can be trusted. The specific forms this confrontation takes change across cultures and centuries — the ancient world framed it differently than the modern one, the person in crisis frames it differently than the person in prosperity — but the underlying structure is consistent: people need to know whether the story they are organizing their lives around is true. Not whether it is inspiring, not whether it is culturally useful, not whether it provides a serviceable framework for navigating daily life, but whether it is actually, historically, verifiably true. This need is not a product of modern skepticism. It is a feature of human consciousness as such, present in every culture that has ever taken its beliefs seriously enough to ask whether they correspond to reality.

The Gospel of Luke begins with this question directly. Its author does not open with genealogy or wilderness or action. He opens with an epistemological claim: I have investigated this carefully, I have consulted those who were eyewitnesses, I have arranged the account in order, and I am writing to you so that you may know the certainty of the things you have been taught. The word translated "certainty" carries the weight of secure, verifiable knowledge — not the certainty of faith alone but the certainty that comes from a carefully ordered account grounded in reliable testimony. Luke is not offering a meditation. He is offering evidence, and the distinction matters for everything that follows.

This opening is unlike anything in the other Gospels. Mark begins mid-action and never pauses to explain itself. Matthew begins with genealogy and expects a reader already inside the tradition. John begins in eternity and speaks in the register of cosmic declaration. Luke alone steps into view before the narrative begins, identifies himself as a writer who has done research, names the process by which the account was assembled, and addresses a specific recipient whose need for certainty is the occasion for the entire work. The prologue is brief — four verses — but it establishes a relationship between author, audience, and subject that governs the entire Gospel: Luke is writing for people who have already encountered the claims of the gospel and need to know whether those claims can bear the weight of genuine investigation.

To understand why Luke frames the work this way requires attending to the situation of the people for whom it was first written. These were not people for whom the gospel was a cultural inheritance absorbed without examination. Many of them had come to faith from outside Judaism, had encountered the claims of the Jesus movement as adult converts, and lived in communities where those claims were contested and where the cost of holding them was real. Theophilus — whose name means "lover of God" and who may be a representative figure as much as a specific individual — is addressed as someone who has been catechized in the faith and now needs the deeper certainty that careful historical account can provide. The gospel this person received was not self-evidently true to the surrounding culture. It required investigation. Luke provides it.

What distinguishes Luke's approach to this question is the seriousness with which it takes the relationship between history and faith. Where the other Gospels make their theological claims through the narrative itself — through the accumulation of episodes, the development of themes, the structure of the whole — Luke makes an explicit methodological claim at the outset: this account is grounded in eyewitness testimony, carefully consulted, ordered with intention. The faith Luke is commending is not a leap away from evidence but a response to it, and the evidence is historical before it is theological. The sequence matters. Luke establishes the historical ground before building the theological argument, because the theological argument depends on the historical ground being solid.

The Weight of What Is Missing

The people who appear in Luke's Gospel are, more consistently than in any other, the people whose absence from the center of religious and social life was taken for granted by the world around them. Women appear earlier, more frequently, and with more narrative significance than in any parallel account. Shepherds receive the first announcement of the birth of the Son of God. A Samaritan — an ethnic and religious outsider whom respectable Jewish society would not have counted as a neighbor — becomes the moral center of the Gospel's most famous parable. Tax collectors and sinners eat with Jesus while the righteous observe from a critical distance. The poor are blessed. The rich are warned. The people at the margins of every available social framework keep appearing at the center of what God is doing.

This is not accidental, and it is not merely the expression of a general preference for the underdog. It is a sustained theological argument pressed through narrative: the kingdom that Jesus announces is not the kingdom that existing social structures have prepared people to expect. The person most positioned to recognize it is not the person most invested in the existing order but the person whose exclusion from that order has left them with nothing to lose by believing something different. This is why the shepherds hear the angels and not the priests. This is why the women are the first witnesses of the resurrection and not the disciples who had been given advance notice. This is why the prodigal's father runs toward the returning son while the elder brother stands at a distance, tallying the cost of a generosity he cannot yet understand.

For modern readers living in communities shaped by the assumption that religious and social access is broadly distributed, the force of Luke's sustained attention to the excluded can require some effort to feel. The effort is worth making. The people Luke keeps placing at the center of the narrative were not sentimental favorites in the first-century world. They were genuinely excluded — from full participation in Temple worship, from legal standing in court, from the social networks that made economic life possible, from the categories of person whose testimony was considered reliable. Luke's insistence on their centrality to the gospel story is not a minor narrative choice. It is a declaration about the character of the God whose story this is, and the declaration has not lost its capacity to disturb every arrangement that has claimed divine sanction while reproducing the exclusions Luke's Jesus consistently dismantles.

The Question of Who Is Included

Luke's Gospel is more consistently and more explicitly concerned with the question of Gentile inclusion than any other. This is not because Luke abandons the Jewish framework of the story — the narrative is saturated with the Hebrew Scriptures, the Temple appears in the first and last chapters, and Jesus is presented throughout as the fulfillment of everything Israel's long story had been moving toward. It is because Luke understands the fulfillment of that story as necessarily universal in its scope. The prophecy that the aged Simeon speaks over the infant Jesus in the Temple is addressed to "all peoples" — a light of revelation to the Gentiles as well as the glory of Israel. The universality is announced before the ministry begins and confirmed at its conclusion, when the risen Jesus commissions his followers to proclaim repentance and forgiveness of sins to all nations.

This concern with inclusion shapes Luke's portrait of Jesus in ways that are visible throughout the narrative. Jesus travels through Samaria when other Jews would have taken the longer route to avoid it. He commends a Samaritan's faith explicitly and publicly. He heals ten lepers and notes with particular emphasis that the one who returned to give thanks was a foreigner. He responds to a Gentile centurion's faith with a declaration that he has not found such faith in all of Israel. These are not isolated incidents. They are a cumulative argument about the reach of the kingdom that Jesus announces — an argument that Luke is making deliberately, with the same ordered intention that he describes in his prologue, in order to produce in his reader the certainty that the gospel is for them, whoever they are, wherever they have come from, whatever has previously excluded them from the story.

The question of inclusion is not merely a first-century question about the relationship between Judaism and the emerging Jesus movement. It is one of the most consistently pressing questions of any era, including the present one. Every community of faith carries within itself the structural tendency to define its boundaries in ways that reproduce the exclusions it was supposed to dissolve, to welcome in principle while creating in practice the conditions that make certain people feel that welcome does not extend to them. Luke's Gospel presses against this tendency with unusual persistence and unusual specificity. The Gospels's sustained attention to who is present in the room when Jesus speaks and who is absent, who eats at the table and who watches from outside, who receives the announcement of good news and who is left to wonder whether it applies to them, is not incidental background. It is the central argument, pressed from every available angle across twenty-four chapters.

The Longing for Genuine Restoration

Luke's Gospel also engages a longing that runs beneath every human life, regardless of cultural context — the longing to return, to be found, to be restored to something that was lost and whose loss has shaped everything since. The three parables of chapter fifteen are the most concentrated expression of this longing in the entire New Testament. The lost sheep. The lost coin. The lost son. Each parable is a variation on the same pattern: something of value is lost, the search is total and determined, the recovery is celebrated with a joy that exceeds what observers think the occasion warrants. The father of the prodigal son does not wait for his returning child to complete the walk home. He sees him while he is still a long way off and runs — runs, in a culture where running was undignified for a man of his age and standing — and embraces him before a word of the prepared speech has been delivered.

The parable is not primarily about forgiveness in the abstract. It is about the specific, physical, running-toward character of the restoration that God offers — a restoration that is not conditional on adequate penitence or appropriate self-presentation but that moves toward the lost before the lost has finished finding its way back. This is the restoration that Luke's Gospel presents as the content of the good news that Jesus announces. It is not primarily a restoration of status or standing within an existing social framework, though it has those implications. It is the restoration of a relationship — the relationship between the human creature and the God who made it, who has been looking down the road since the departure, who runs at the first sight of return.

The longing for this restoration is not exclusive to first-century Palestine or to communities shaped by Jewish messianic hope. It is a feature of human experience in every cultural context and every historical period. The specific forms in which it expresses itself vary enormously — in some cultures it takes explicitly religious form, in others it surfaces as the inarticulate sense that something essential has been lost and that the life currently being lived is a diminished version of what life was meant to be. Luke's Gospel speaks to this longing with unusual directness precisely because it does not dress the restoration in the language of deserving. The prodigal son does not earn his way home. He comes to himself, he rises, he returns, and his father runs to meet him. The restoration precedes the speech. The embrace precedes the explanation. This is the shape of the good news that Luke has carefully investigated, ordered, and written down so that his reader may know its certainty.

The Shape of What Follows

These dimensions — the concern for historical certainty, the sustained attention to the excluded, the insistence on universal inclusion, and the portrait of restoration that moves toward the lost before they have finished returning — are not separate topics that Luke handles in separate sections. They are angles on a single claim that the Gospel develops from its prologue to its final scene on the road to Emmaus, where two disciples who do not yet know they are in the presence of the risen Jesus find their hearts burning within them as the Scriptures are opened to them. The breadth of Luke's narrative is the formal expression of the breadth of the claim it carries: something has happened in the person of Jesus that cannot be confined within any of the categories that were available before it happened, and the response it requires is open to everyone.

The chapters that follow examine the historical world that shaped Luke's account, the literary structure that organizes its argument, the major themes that run from the annunciation to the ascension, the ways the Gospel has been misread across centuries of reception, and the specific ways it continues to address the lives of people who encounter it seriously. The goal throughout is not to make Luke easier to receive but to make it possible to receive it more fully — to remove the obstacles that can prevent a modern reader from engaging the text as the sustained, carefully ordered, pastorally attentive document it is. Luke was written by someone who took the craft of writing seriously enough to say so at the outset. Reading it well requires the same seriousness in return. The chapters that follow are an attempt to make that engagement possible.

Chapter 2

Orientation

"With this in mind, since I myself have carefully investigated
everything from the beginning, I too decided to write an orderly
account for you, most excellent Theophilus."
— Luke 1:3

A Gospel for a Community Finding Its Footing

The historical circumstances that produced Luke's Gospel are not
background information to be acknowledged and set aside. They
are the conditions that explain why the Gospel sounds the way it
does — why its opening is self-conscious and methodological
rather than urgent and plunging, why its portrait of Jesus is so
consistently attentive to those the surrounding world had
excluded, why it moves with the deliberate pace of a writer who is
not racing against time but building a case that must be able to
bear weight. Luke is a document shaped at every level by the
specific situation of communities that had received the gospel
from outside their own tradition and needed to understand what
they had received well enough to hold it with confidence in a
world that did not share it.

Luke was almost certainly composed in the late first century,
most likely in the 80s CE, making it one of the later Gospels. The
community for which it was written was not navigating the acute
crisis of Neronian persecution that shaped Mark, nor the intense
internal debate with the synagogue that shaped Matthew. It was
navigating a different and in some ways more complex challenge:
the question of what it meant to be the people of God in the
extended period between the resurrection and the return — a

period that was proving longer than many had anticipated, in communities increasingly populated by Gentile converts who had no prior Jewish formation and for whom the Hebrew Scriptures were not inherited tradition but newly encountered text.

This context illuminates Luke's distinctive treatment of time in ways that careful reading makes visible. The Gospel is less concerned with the urgency of the immediately impending end than with the faithful ordering of life in a present that is going to continue for a while. The parable of the ten minas, unique to Luke, explicitly addresses a community that has been given resources and instructed to put them to use during the master's absence rather than simply waiting for the return. The extended travel narrative that dominates chapters nine through nineteen is not merely geographical. It is a sustained meditation on what discipleship looks like during the long middle of the story — when the founding events are receding into the past and the consummation remains ahead and the community must find its way through the present without either abandoning the past or collapsing the distance to the future.

The Gentile context, if accurate, also gives Luke's sustained attention to universal inclusion its specific pastoral gravity. Communities living in the Greco-Roman world without prior Jewish formation needed to understand not only what the gospel claimed but where they fit in the story it was telling. Luke's portrait of a Jesus who moves consistently toward Samaritans, Gentiles, the ritually impure, and the socially excluded was not a generic spiritual claim about divine generosity. It was a direct and specific assurance that the story being told had always been moving toward them — that the God of Israel was not a tribal deity whose grace was distributed through ethnic membership but the God of all peoples, whose purposes had always been larger than any single community's inheritance.

Who Wrote Luke and When

The Gospel does not identify its author within the text. The attribution to Luke is traditional, drawn from early church testimony that consistently names him as a physician and companion of Paul — the figure who appears by name in three of the Pauline letters and who is described in Colossians as the beloved physician. The tradition connecting the Gospel to this Luke is early enough and consistent enough to carry weight, even in the absence of internal identification. The "we" passages in Acts, where the narrative shifts unexpectedly to first-person plural during certain portions of Paul's missionary journeys, have been read by many interpreters as the traces of an eyewitness travel companion whose presence is encoded in the pronoun rather than announced directly.

What internal evidence establishes is that the author was a person of genuine literary sophistication writing for an audience that shared that sophistication. The prologue is the most explicit signal: its formal conventions, its appeal to eyewitness sources, its stated concern for ordered arrangement and verifiable certainty — these are the conventions of Hellenistic historiography, and their deployment in the opening four verses positions the Gospel within a recognizable literary tradition whose implied readers were educated people accustomed to evaluating historical claims by explicit methodological criteria. This is not the audience Mark wrote for. It is not primarily the audience Matthew wrote for. Luke is addressing people who approach historical narrative with the evaluative habits of the educated Greco-Roman world, and he meets them there before he asks them to follow him anywhere else.

Most scholars place the composition between 80 and 90 CE. The primary evidence is the literary relationship with Mark — Luke clearly knows and uses Mark as a source — and the apparent awareness of Jerusalem's destruction in 70 CE, which Luke's version of the eschatological discourse treats with more historical specificity than Mark's parallel. The use of a named source, the degree of literary polish, and the evident concern with the long-term shape of community life all suggest a document composed at some distance from the founding events, by a writer who had access to multiple sources and the literary skill to weave them into a sustained and coherent argument.

The Structure of the Gospel

Luke is organized around a geographical and theological movement that gives the entire narrative its shape and its momentum. Jerusalem is the destination from the beginning and the center of the conclusion. The Gospel opens in the Temple, where Zechariah receives the announcement of John's birth. It ends in Jerusalem, where the disciples are instructed to wait for the promise of the Father before they go anywhere. Between these two Temple moments, everything in the narrative is oriented toward Jerusalem — first as the destination Jesus sets his face toward at the beginning of the long central section, then as the city he weeps over on his approach, then as the place where everything culminates in the passion, resurrection, and ascension.

The structure within this overarching movement falls into recognizable phases. The infancy narrative of chapters one and two is unique to Luke and establishes the theological stakes of the entire story through a series of announcements, births, songs, and Temple encounters that locate Jesus within the longest arc of Israel's hope. The Galilean ministry of chapters three through nine establishes Jesus' identity through a combination of proclamation and demonstration, culminating in the transfiguration and the turn toward Jerusalem. The travel narrative of chapters nine through nineteen is the longest and most distinctive section of the Gospel — a sustained journey toward the city that organizes a vast collection of teaching, parable, and encounter that has no precise parallel in the other Gospels. The passion, resurrection, and ascension of chapters nineteen through twenty-four bring the narrative to its conclusion and open the horizon that Acts will follow.

Within this structure, Luke employs several distinctive literary techniques. The most characteristic is his use of parallel narratives and paired episodes — a technique that operates across large distances in the text and requires the reader to hold earlier material in mind when encountering later development. The annunciation to Mary is paired with the annunciation to Zechariah, and the comparison illuminates both. The healing of the centurion's servant is paired with the raising of the widow's son at Nain, and together they press the claim about who receives the mercy of God. The three parables of chapter fifteen function as a single sustained argument pressed from three different angles. Luke structures his material through accumulation and pairing in ways that require the reader to attend not only to individual episodes but to the patterns that emerge from their arrangement.

Luke's Sources

Luke does not appear to have composed his Gospel without reference to earlier material, and unlike the other Evangelists, he says so explicitly. His prologue acknowledges that many have already undertaken to compile accounts of the things that have been accomplished, and that he himself has investigated everything from the beginning. The two-source hypothesis that accounts for the literary relationships among the Synoptic Gospels identifies Mark as the earliest Gospel and one of Luke's primary narrative sources. The evidence is substantial: Luke follows Mark's narrative sequence through much of the Galilean ministry, his versions of shared material tend to polish Mark's rougher Greek, and he consistently incorporates Markan episodes into a framework that organizes them toward his own theological purposes.

Beyond Mark, Luke shares with Matthew a substantial body of teaching material — sayings and discourses of Jesus that do not appear in Mark — which scholars conventionally refer to as Q. The relationship between Luke's use of this material and Matthew's is complex: the two Evangelists arrange the same sayings in different sequences, embed them in different narrative contexts, and sometimes present them with significant verbal variation. Luke's arrangement tends to distribute this material across the travel narrative rather than collecting it into sustained discourse blocks, which has the effect of integrating Jesus' teaching into the movement of the story rather than pausing the narrative for extended instruction.

What makes Luke distinctive among the Synoptics is the material that appears in neither Mark nor Matthew. The infancy narrative is entirely Luke's own. The parables of the Good Samaritan, the Prodigal Son, the Rich Man and Lazarus, the Pharisee and the Tax Collector, and numerous others appear only here. The stories of Zacchaeus, the ten lepers, the widow of Nain, the sinful woman who anoints Jesus' feet — these are Luke's unique contribution to the portrait of Jesus in the Gospels. What this material shares is a consistent concern with precisely the people who appear at the margins of the other Gospels' narratives: women, Gentiles, the poor, the ritually excluded, the morally compromised. This is not an accident. It is the signature of a writer who has investigated the tradition with a specific question in mind: who does this Jesus actually go to, and what does that say about the God he represents?

Luke's Portrait of Jesus

The Christological portrait Luke develops is constructed through a distinctive combination of titles, demonstrations, and the sustained attention to prayer that runs through the entire Gospel. Jesus is the Son of God — declared at the annunciation, confirmed at the baptism, tested in the wilderness, confessed by the demons before any human character understands it. He is the Christ — the anointed one whose identity Peter confesses at Caesarea Philippi and whose meaning Luke has been carefully establishing from the moment the angels announced his birth to the shepherds. He is the Son of Man — the title Jesus uses most consistently in his own speech, carrying the Danielic resonance of both present humility and future coming in glory. He is Lord — the title that Luke uses more frequently than any other Synoptic Evangelist, which carries its full weight as the title of the one to whom ultimate allegiance is owed.

Alongside these titles, Luke preserves a portrait of Jesus that is distinctively characterized by prayer. Jesus prays at his baptism. He prays before choosing the twelve. He prays at the transfiguration. He prays in Gethsemane. He prays from the cross. The pattern is consistent across the entire Gospel: before every major event, at every pivotal moment, Jesus is at prayer. This is not incidental detail. It is a constitutive element of Luke's portrait — the evidence that the authority Jesus exercises is not self-generated but received, that the mission he carries is not his own initiative but his Father's commission, that the relationship between the Son and the Father is the ground on which everything else in the narrative stands. Luke's Jesus is the one who teaches his disciples to pray because prayer is not a religious technique he endorses but the reality his own life is organized around.

Luke also preserves a portrait of Jesus that is more consistently joyful than any other Gospel. This is not the exuberant, untroubled joy of a narrative that has not looked honestly at suffering — Luke contains Gethsemane, the weeping over Jerusalem, the darkness of the cross. It is the deep joy of a narrative in which the return of the lost is always cause for celebration disproportionate to what observers think the occasion warrants. The father runs. The woman calls her neighbors. The shepherd lifts the sheep onto his shoulders. The disciples return from their mission with joy, and Jesus himself rejoices in the Holy Spirit. The note of joy that Luke sounds again and again is not emotional coloring applied to a story that could have been told without it. It is a theological claim about the character of the God who is acting in Jesus — a God for whom the finding of the lost is always worth more than the maintenance of the found.

The Role of Women in Luke

No dimension of Luke is more immediately striking to careful readers than its sustained and unprecedented attention to women. They appear in the infancy narrative with full theological agency: Mary receives the annunciation and responds with a theological declaration that shapes the entire Gospel's understanding of reversal and restoration. Elizabeth confirms what the angel has said. Anna the prophetess speaks of the child to all who are waiting for redemption in Jerusalem. Women accompany Jesus throughout his ministry, providing for him out of their own resources — an economic arrangement Luke names explicitly and the other Gospels do not. Women are present at the cross when the male disciples have scattered. Women are the first witnesses of the resurrection and the first commissioned to announce it.

The portrait is not merely quantitative. Luke gives women narrative significance at every level of the story that the surrounding culture had systematically denied them. In a world where women's testimony was not legally credible, Luke places women at the most crucial moment of evidentiary claim in the entire gospel: the empty tomb. In a world where women's religious formation was considered secondary and their access to sacred spaces restricted, Luke has Mary sitting at Jesus' feet in the posture of a disciple receiving instruction — and has Jesus defend this against the complaint that she has abandoned her proper role. In a world where women were defined primarily by their relationships to men, Luke gives them names, histories, and voices of their own.

This sustained attention to women is not unrelated to Luke's broader concern with the excluded. It is one of its most concentrated expressions — the application of the same theological logic to the specific exclusion that organized the social world most completely: the exclusion of half the human race from full participation in the religious and public life of the culture. Luke's Gospel does not address this exclusion with a systematic argument about gender equality. It addresses it by showing Jesus repeatedly in the company of women, receiving their ministry, commending their faith, telling stories in which they are the protagonists, and entrusting them with the most significant witness in human history. The argument is made through narrative, as Luke's most important arguments always are.

Preparing to Read Luke Well

Understanding the historical context of Luke's composition, the community for which it was written, the sources the author drew upon and acknowledged, the structural features that organize its movement toward Jerusalem and beyond, the portrait of Jesus characterized by prayer and joy and consistent movement toward the excluded, the unprecedented attention to women as theological agents in the story — all of these are forms of orientation that prepare the reader to engage the text itself more fully and to receive its argument more completely.

But orientation is preparation, not replacement. The goal of everything this chapter has described is to clear away the obstacles that prevent a modern reader from engaging Luke directly — the sense that its literary polish is ornamental rather than purposeful, that its attention to the marginalized is sentimental rather than theological, that its portrait of Jesus at prayer is a devotional detail rather than a structural claim. When those obstacles are cleared, what remains is the text itself: a carefully researched, deliberately ordered, pastorally attentive document whose author took seriously enough to explain what he was doing before he began doing it.

Luke rewards the reader who brings the same care to reading it that its author brought to writing it. Its length is not padding but density — there is more happening in its twenty-four chapters than any single reading can fully draw out. The reader who returns to it across different seasons of life, who allows the travel narrative to press its teaching about discipleship in the long middle of the story, who brings the experience of being excluded or including to a text that has always known about both, will consistently find that Luke has more to say than any previous reading has exhausted. The orientation this chapter provides is the beginning of that engagement, not its completion. The text itself, read with sustained attention and honest openness, is where the certainty Theophilus was promised becomes available to every reader who comes to Luke willing to receive it.

Chapter 3

The World Behind the Book

*"The Spirit of the Lord is on me, because he has anointed me to
proclaim good news to the poor."*
— Luke 4:18

The Greco-Roman World Luke Inhabited

The world that produced Luke's Gospel was shaped by two forces
whose intersection was at once generative and deeply unstable:
Roman imperial power and the wide variety of religious and
philosophical traditions that populated the Mediterranean basin.
Rome provided the administrative architecture — taxation,
military presence, legal frameworks, the roads and shipping lanes
that connected the known world into a single economic system.
But for the communities Luke was writing for, the more
immediate context was the bewildering plurality of the Greco-
Roman religious marketplace: mystery cults, philosophical schools,
imperial religion, local deities, and the increasingly visible and
increasingly strange communities of people who worshipped the
God of Israel and, stranger still, a crucified Jew from an
insignificant province whom they called Lord.

Luke writes into this world with more explicit awareness of it
than any other Evangelist. His prologue adopts the conventions of
Hellenistic historiography. His infancy narrative echoes the literary
patterns of Greco-Roman birth announcements of great figures.
His parables deploy the social textures of the Mediterranean world
— landlords and tenants, traveling merchants, women managing
households, wealthy men hosting banquets — with a specificity
that assumes an audience that recognizes these textures from daily

experience. Luke is not translating Jewish categories into Greco-Roman form for an audience that would otherwise miss the point. He is writing a Gospel that inhabits the Greco-Roman world as native territory while insisting that the story it tells is the decisive event toward which all of history, including Greco-Roman history, has been moving.

Rome generally maintained its administrative tolerance of subject religions that posed no threat to public order, but the toleration was conditional and its conditions were enforced. The imperial cult — the worship of the emperor and the Roman state as divine — created a particular tension for communities that made absolute claims about the lordship of Jesus. In the cities of the empire, civic life was saturated with religious practice: public sacrifice, festivals, guild meals that began with offerings to patron deities, official ceremonies that wove together political and religious obligation in ways that made conscientious non-participation both socially costly and economically consequential. The communities for whom Luke wrote were navigating these pressures daily, and the Gospel's consistent insistence that Jesus is Lord — not Caesar, not the local deity, not the patron of the guild — was not a theological abstraction. It was a claim with concrete daily implications for how one lived in a world organized around different loyalties.

The Economic Landscape

The economic conditions of the first-century Mediterranean world are directly relevant to Luke's narrative in ways that his sustained attention to wealth, poverty, and the social effects of economic inequality makes impossible to miss. Luke mentions money and possessions more than any other Gospel. The rich man who builds bigger barns, the dishonest manager, the rich man who ignores Lazarus at his gate, Zacchaeus the wealthy tax collector, the widow who gives her two coins, the prodigal who squanders his inheritance — these are not illustrations chosen randomly from available cultural material. They are concentrated attention to the economic fault line that ran through every community Luke was writing for and that the gospel he was commending addressed with unusual directness.

Wealth in the Greco-Roman world was organized around a system of patronage that structured virtually every significant social relationship. The wealthy patron provided resources, legal protection, and social access to clients who in return provided loyalty, public honor, and political support. This system was not peripheral to social life. It was the architecture of social life, the framework within which everything from business transactions to marriage arrangements to civic participation was organized. To be without a patron was to be genuinely vulnerable — exposed to the legal system without protection, unable to access markets without connections, dependent on the charity of neighbors whose own margins were often thin.

Into this world, Luke's Jesus announces good news to the poor — not as a spiritual metaphor for the humble but as a concrete declaration that the kingdom he proclaims reorganizes the patronage relationships that determine who has access to what. The reversals that Mary's Magnificat announces in chapter one — the mighty brought down from their thrones, the hungry filled with good things — are not merely eschatological promises about a distant future. They are descriptions of what the kingdom's arrival looks like in the specific social and economic arrangements of the communities where it takes root. The sharing of possessions that characterizes the early community in Acts, the sequel to Luke's Gospel, is the social form that the kingdom's economic logic takes when it is received seriously by people who live in a world structured around the accumulation and protection of advantage.

The World of the Synagogue and Torah

By the first century, the synagogue had become the primary institution of Jewish communal life throughout the diaspora — the place where Torah was read and interpreted, where the community gathered weekly, where Jewish identity was formed and maintained in the midst of the surrounding Gentile culture. Luke's Jesus is consistently presented as someone who participates in this institutional life: he reads from the scroll in the Nazareth synagogue, he teaches in synagogues throughout Galilee, he engages the scribal tradition with the fluency of someone formed within it. The conflict that develops between Jesus and the synagogue authorities is not a conflict between an outsider and an institution he never belonged to. It is the conflict that develops within an institution when someone inside it presses its own claims beyond the limits the institution's custodians are prepared to accept.

The Torah in Luke's narrative is not a burden to be lightened or a system to be replaced. It is the framework within which Jesus operates and the tradition he consistently claims to be fulfilling. When Jesus reads from Isaiah in the Nazareth synagogue and announces that the Scripture is fulfilled in their hearing, he is not announcing the obsolescence of what he has just read. He is claiming that the vision it describes — good news to the poor, release to the captives, recovery of sight to the blind, the year of the Lord's favor — is not a future hope but a present reality inaugurated by his own person and ministry. The conflict is about the scope of the fulfillment and the identity of those who are included within it, not about whether the Torah's vision was worth fulfilling.

This context illuminates one of Luke's most distinctive narrative choices: the consistent presentation of Jesus in conversation with Torah experts who are either hostile, genuinely curious, or quietly sympathetic. The Pharisees who warn Jesus about Herod, the lawyer who asks what must be done to inherit eternal life, the ruler who addresses Jesus as good teacher — these are not caricatures of religious hypocrisy. They are people formed within a serious intellectual tradition who are encountering something that their tradition has not prepared them to categorize, and whose responses range across the full spectrum of what that encounter produces. Luke's treatment of these figures is more nuanced than any other Gospel's, and the nuance is itself an argument about the relationship between the tradition Jesus inhabits and the fulfillment he announces.

The Gentile Religious Landscape

The Gentile world into which Luke's communities were set was not a world without religion. It was a world saturated with religious practice, organized around a plurality of deities whose domains and personalities were well established, whose rituals structured the rhythms of daily and civic life, and whose expectations of their worshippers were primarily behavioral rather than exclusive. The exclusive claim of the God of Israel — that no other gods were to be honored, that loyalty to this God was not compatible with participation in the religious practices that organized the surrounding culture — was one of the features that made Jewish communities in the diaspora both distinctive and difficult to fully integrate into civic life.

The communities for whom Luke wrote included people who had come from this religious world, who had been worshippers of the gods their families had worshipped for generations, and who had encountered the claims of the Jesus movement and found them persuasive enough to accept at real social cost. These were not people with no prior religious formation. They were people whose prior religious formation had not prepared them for the specific claims the gospel made: that there was one God, that this God had acted decisively in the history of a specific people, that the culmination of that action was the life, death, and resurrection of a specific person, and that the appropriate response was the exclusive loyalty that the surrounding culture regarded as antisocial and the Jewish community had always known was costly.

Luke's attention to the Gentile world shapes several of the Gospel's most distinctive narrative choices. The parable of the Good Samaritan is not merely a story about neighborliness. It is a deliberate provocation that places a despised ethnic and religious outsider in the position of moral exemplar in a conversation with a Torah expert about the requirements of the law. The healing of the ten lepers, in which only the Samaritan returns to give thanks, presses the same point from a different angle: the one least expected to recognize what has happened is the one who responds most completely to it. These are not incidental choices. They are the concentrated expression of Luke's sustained theological argument that the boundaries separating Israel from the nations have been crossed from within by the one whose fulfillment of Israel's vocation opens its promise to all peoples.

Honor, Shame, and the Social World

The social world of the first-century Mediterranean was organized around the values of honor and shame in ways that shaped every significant relationship and every public interaction. Honor was not primarily a psychological condition. It was a social resource — as real and as practically consequential as money, essential to participation in the economic, legal, and civic networks that made ordinary life possible. Its absence or removal was not merely an emotional wound. It was a practical catastrophe that could destroy a person's ability to function in every domain of public life. The management of honor — its accumulation, its protection, its public display, and the response to its challenge — was one of the central preoccupations of social life at every level of the culture.

This context illuminates the social dimensions of Luke's narrative in ways that a reading focused primarily on the spiritual or theological can miss entirely. When the prodigal son's father runs to meet him while he is still a long way off, the detail that he runs is not incidental local color. In the honor-shame culture of the Mediterranean world, a man of standing did not run in public. Running was undignified. The father's running is itself a deliberate act of self-humiliation undertaken to spare his returning son the gauntlet of public shame he would otherwise face walking back through the village that knew what he had done. The embrace and the robe and the ring and the feast are not simply expressions of joy. They are the public rehabilitation of a person whose honor had been destroyed by his own choices, accomplished by the father's willingness to absorb the shame that the restoration required.

The consistent attention Luke pays to the reversal of honor and shame throughout the Gospel is not a general preference for the humble over the proud. It is a sustained theological argument about the character of the God whose kingdom Jesus announces — a God who runs toward the shamed rather than waiting for them to restore themselves to eligibility for approach, who invites to the feast those who have no social standing to deserve the invitation, who commends the tax collector's prayer over the Pharisee's precisely because the tax collector makes no claim to the honor that the surrounding culture would acknowledge. Every reversal of honor and shame in Luke is an enacted description of what the kingdom's arrival looks like in a world organized around those values.

The Lives of Women in Luke's World

The situation of women in the first-century Mediterranean world was defined by legal, economic, and social constraints that were both pervasive and largely taken for granted by the culture that maintained them. Women were under the legal authority of their fathers until marriage and of their husbands thereafter. Their testimony was not considered legally credible. Their access to education, to public religious leadership, and to the economic networks that organized male social life was systematically restricted. Their value was defined primarily in terms of the roles they performed within the household — wife, mother, manager of domestic life — and their public reputation depended almost entirely on the sexual honor of the household they belonged to.

Within these constraints, women in the first century exercised genuine agency and genuine influence in domains that the formal legal and social structures did not reach. The management of the household, which was simultaneously an economic enterprise and a social unit, required real skill and real authority. Women's networks of relationship operated in parallel to men's and served many of the same social functions. Religious practice within the household was substantially in women's hands. In Jewish communities, the formation of children in Torah was a domestic responsibility that fell primarily to mothers. In Gentile communities, the religious character of the household reflected the religious commitments of those who managed it, and women's conversions to new religious movements frequently preceded their households' conversions.

It is precisely this world that Luke's Gospel consistently challenges and reimagines. The women who travel with Jesus and provide for him out of their own resources are exercising the economic agency their culture permitted them while using it in the service of a movement whose values challenged the social order that constrained them. Mary who sits at Jesus' feet in the posture of a disciple is doing something that the surrounding culture would have regarded as a violation of the appropriate ordering of domestic and religious life, and Jesus' defense of her choice is simultaneously a pastoral judgment about this specific moment and a broader claim about the kind of learning that the kingdom calls every person to pursue regardless of the social categories that have defined what learning is for whom. The women at the tomb, whose testimony the male disciples initially dismiss as an idle tale, are the first witnesses to the central claim on which the entire gospel rests. Luke knows the culture's verdict on their credibility. He places them at the center of the evidence anyway.

A World of Movement and Encounter

The world of Luke's narrative is also a world defined by movement. Jesus is constantly traveling: from Galilee toward Jerusalem along the central travel narrative of chapters nine through nineteen, through villages and towns, across social boundaries, into homes where dinner table encounters become occasions for the most searching teaching in the Gospel. The road is not merely a narrative device. It is the social space where the unexpected meeting happens, where the Samaritan stops while the priest and the Levite pass by, where two disciples walking toward Emmaus encounter the risen Jesus without recognizing him and find their hearts burning within them as he opens the Scriptures. Luke's Gospel is a Gospel of encounter on the road, and the road is always the space where the boundaries that organize settled life become permeable.

The dinner table is Luke's other distinctive social space. More than any other Evangelist, Luke places Jesus at meals — eating with Pharisees, with tax collectors, with sinners, with the disciples, with the two at Emmaus who recognize him in the breaking of the bread. The meal in the ancient world was one of the most socially structured contexts of daily life: who ate with whom, where they reclined, what they were served, who served them — all of these details communicated social information about hierarchy, inclusion, and relationship. Jesus' table fellowship in Luke consistently violates the social logic that organizes these arrangements, and the violations are not accidental. They are the enacted form of the kingdom's claim that the boundaries determining who belongs together have been redrawn by the one who hosts the feast.

A World Defined by Longing

The world behind Luke is finally a world in which the longing for something more adequate than the present order can provide runs beneath every surface Luke's narrative touches. The longing of Israel for the fulfillment of its prophetic promises is present from the first chapter, where Zechariah and Elizabeth and Mary and Simeon and Anna are all described as people who have been waiting — waiting for the consolation of Israel, waiting for the redemption of Jerusalem, waiting for the one who was to come. The longing of the Gentile world for a religious framework adequate to the human situation is present in the God-fearers who appear at the edges of Jewish community life, drawn to the ethical seriousness and the monotheistic clarity of Jewish faith without having taken the step of full conversion. The longing of the poor for a different order of things than the one that has placed them at the bottom of every structure that organizes access to what makes human life possible is present in the crowds who gather to hear Jesus in the villages of Galilee and the streets of Jerusalem.

Luke's Gospel inhabits this longing without exploiting it. It does not offer easy comfort or quick resolution to situations that have been shaped by centuries of economic, social, and political forces that do not change easily or quickly. It offers a Jesus who announces that the year of the Lord's favor has arrived, who demonstrates what that announcement means in the specific lives of specific people at the specific margins where the world's longing is most acute, and who presses toward a Jerusalem where the longing will be addressed in the most costly and most comprehensive way possible. This is the world behind the book — not a world of settled clarity but a world of genuine and multifaceted longing, met by a gospel whose scope is as wide as the longing and whose cost is as real as the world that generated it.

Chapter 4

The Story or Flow of the Book

"He said to them, 'This is what I told you while I was still with you: Everything must be fulfilled that is written about me in the Law of Moses, the Prophets and the Psalms.'"
— Luke 24:44

The Shape of Luke's Narrative

Luke unfolds as a story with a destination and a sequel. Every element of its structure — the carefully composed prologue, the infancy narrative that establishes the theological stakes, the Galilean ministry that demonstrates Jesus' identity, the long journey toward Jerusalem that organizes the bulk of the Gospel's teaching, the passion and resurrection, and the ascension that opens the horizon toward Acts — serves the movement toward and through the cross and out toward the ends of the earth. The narrative does not meander. It moves with the deliberate purposefulness of a writer who announced in his opening four verses that he was composing an ordered account, and who has organized twenty-four chapters to carry an argument that only the whole can complete.

The theological architecture of this movement is as important as its narrative momentum. Luke is not simply recording what happened in the sequence it occurred. He is constructing an argument about who Jesus is, what his coming means for the full range of human beings who have been excluded from the story, and what the life organized around his kingdom looks like in the extended present between resurrection and return. The argument is embedded in the narrative structure itself — in what is placed in parallel with what, in which episodes are unique to Luke and why, in the sustained attention to prayer and joy and reversal that runs as a current beneath every surface of the story. Reading Luke as a sequence of familiar passages misses the argument that only the whole can carry.

The structure of the Gospel falls into five recognizable phases, each with its own character and its own contribution to the overall movement. The infancy narrative establishes the theological context before a word of public ministry has been spoken. The Galilean ministry demonstrates the character of the one who has come. The travel narrative develops the implications of that character for the community that follows him. The Jerusalem section presses those implications to their most costly and most concentrated expression. And the resurrection and ascension open the story toward the future that Acts will narrate. None of these phases is fully intelligible without the others. The infancy narrative makes claims that the passion narrative fulfills. The travel narrative prepares the reader for demands that only the passion makes fully legible. The ascension closes the Gospel by opening a door that only Acts can walk through.

The Infancy Narrative

The opening two chapters of Luke are unlike anything in the other Gospels, and their distinctive character is not ornamental. Luke begins before the ministry begins, before the public announcement in the Nazareth synagogue, before the baptism and the temptation and the call of the first disciples. He begins with annunciations and births and songs and a Temple encounter, because the theological stakes of everything that follows must be established before the narrative of Jesus' public life can be understood in their full weight. Zechariah and Elizabeth, Mary and Joseph, Simeon and Anna — these are the figures through whom Luke sets the entire Gospel within the longest available arc of Israel's waiting and hope.

The parallel structure of the annunciation to Zechariah and the annunciation to Mary is the first instance of the paired-narrative technique that Luke will use throughout the Gospel. The comparison is precise and deliberate: both receive angelic announcements, both respond with a question, both are given a sign. But the differences illuminate the theological argument Luke is making as clearly as the parallels. Zechariah is a priest in the Temple, a figure of institutional religious authority who has been waiting faithfully and who responds to the announcement with doubt that earns him silence. Mary is a young woman from Nazareth with no institutional standing who responds to an announcement far more startling with a question about mechanism — how will this be? — and then with a submission that becomes the theological ground of everything Luke builds on top of it.

The songs that punctuate the infancy narrative are not decorative interludes. They are compressed theological arguments that establish the interpretive framework for the entire Gospel. Mary's Magnificat announces the reversals that the kingdom's arrival produces: the proud scattered, the mighty brought low, the humble lifted, the hungry filled, the rich sent away empty. These are not polite spiritual metaphors. They are declarations about the direction in which the gospel moves and the social order it disturbs when it is genuinely received. Zechariah's Benedictus announces the fulfillment of the Abrahamic covenant and the dawn of a new age. Simeon's Nunc Dimittis names the scope: a light of revelation to the Gentiles and the glory of Israel. The theological range of the entire Gospel — from the margins of Israel to the ends of the earth — is announced in the Temple before Jesus has spoken a word.

The Galilean Ministry

The transition from infancy narrative to public ministry is marked by the baptism, the genealogy, and the temptation, each of which establishes a dimension of Jesus' identity before the Galilean ministry begins. The genealogy in Luke runs backward from Jesus to Adam — not forward from Abraham as in Matthew — which is itself a structural claim about the scope of what Jesus represents. Matthew's genealogy places Jesus within Israel's story. Luke's places him within the human story as such, the son of Adam, the son of God, the one whose significance is not bounded by ethnic or covenantal category.

The programmatic moment of the Galilean ministry is the reading in the Nazareth synagogue. Jesus unrolls the scroll of Isaiah, reads the passage about the anointed one sent to proclaim good news to the poor, and announces that the Scripture is fulfilled in their hearing. This is Luke's equivalent of Mark's opening proclamation — the moment where the agenda of the entire ministry is announced before the ministry has properly begun. And the agenda is specific: good news to the poor, release to the captives, recovery of sight to the blind, freedom for the oppressed, the year of the Lord's favor. The programmatic nature of the passage is underlined by what immediately follows: the crowd's admiration turns to rage when Jesus suggests that the fulfillment of this program will not be confined to his own people, citing Elijah's provision for a Gentile widow and Elisha's healing of a Syrian commander as precedents for the mission's scope.

The Galilean ministry that follows develops the implications of the Nazareth announcement through a sustained pattern of proclamation and demonstration. Jesus heals the sick, casts out demons, raises the dead, forgives sins, eats with tax collectors and sinners, and responds to John's disciples' question about whether he is the one who was to come with a list that echoes the Isaiah passage: the blind see, the lame walk, the lepers are cleansed, the deaf hear, the dead are raised, and the poor have good news proclaimed to them. Each of these is both a concrete act of restoration and a demonstration of the kingdom's character — what the arrival of God's reign looks like when it touches specific lives in specific conditions of diminishment.

The Travel Narrative

The most distinctive and most extensive structural feature of Luke's Gospel is the travel narrative that stretches from chapter nine through chapter nineteen — ten chapters organized around Jesus' journey toward Jerusalem, a journey he sets his face toward at the beginning of chapter nine and does not complete until chapter nineteen. This is the longest sustained section of the Gospel and the most theologically dense. It contains the Good Samaritan, the Mary and Martha episode, the Lord's Prayer, the three parables of chapter fifteen, Zacchaeus, and dozens of other encounters and teachings that appear only in Luke. It is also the most loosely organized section in terms of obvious narrative progression, and that looseness is itself part of its argument.

The travel narrative is not primarily a geographical account of a journey from Galilee to Judea. It is a sustained meditation on what discipleship looks like in the long middle of the story — when the destination is known but not yet reached, when the cost of following is becoming clearer but has not yet been fully paid, when the community must organize its life around the values of the kingdom in circumstances that have not yet been transformed by the kingdom's full arrival. The journey structure provides a framework for an enormous amount of teaching without requiring the narrative to pretend that it is building toward a specific dramatic climax at each stage. The teaching accumulates as the journey continues, and the accumulation is the point: discipleship in Luke is a long walk, not a single decisive moment.

The parables unique to Luke are concentrated in this section, and their concentration is not accidental. The Good Samaritan redefines the boundary of neighbor in response to a Torah expert's question about eternal life. The friend at midnight presses the community toward persistence in prayer. The rich fool warns against the organization of life around the accumulation of what cannot finally be held. The three parables of chapter fifteen — the lost sheep, the lost coin, the prodigal son — press from three angles the single claim that the God whose kingdom Jesus announces is a God who seeks the lost before they have found their way back, who celebrates recovery with a joy that exceeds what observers think the occasion warrants. These parables are not illustrations of general truths. They are the travel narrative's most concentrated arguments about the character of the God toward whose city the journey is moving.

Jerusalem and the Passion

The entry into Jerusalem opens the final confrontation section of the Gospel. Jesus approaches the city weeping — an emotional moment unique to Luke, which presses the theological weight of the entire narrative into a single image: the one who has come to bring the city its peace weeps because it has not recognized the time of its visitation. The cleansing of the Temple, the controversies with the chief priests and scribes and elders, the eschatological discourse on the Mount of Olives — these develop the conflict that has been building across the entire Gospel and press it toward its resolution in the passion.

The passion narrative in Luke carries several features that distinguish it from the parallel accounts in Mark and Matthew. Jesus' words from the cross in Luke are different: there is no cry of dereliction. Instead, he prays for those who are crucifying him, promises paradise to the repentant criminal who dies beside him, and commends his spirit into his Father's hands. These are not minor variations in detail. They are Luke's sustained theological argument about what the cross means — not the darkness of abandonment but the costly expression of the same forgiveness and inclusion that have characterized the entire ministry. The one who ate with sinners in Galilee dies beside a criminal in Jerusalem and extends to him the same welcome he extended to Zacchaeus in Jericho. The pattern does not change. The cost of maintaining it simply reaches its maximum.

The criminal's response to Jesus from his own cross is one of the most theologically concentrated moments in the entire Gospel. He rebukes the other criminal's mockery, acknowledges his own guilt, and asks only to be remembered when Jesus comes into his kingdom. The response he receives — today you will be with me in paradise — is the most direct statement of immediate salvation in any of the Gospels and a concentrated expression of Luke's consistent theological argument: the one who has nothing to offer, who has no claim on inclusion, who has run out of time for any kind of subsequent performance, is received by the one who moves toward the lost before they have finished finding their way back.

Resurrection and the Road to Emmaus

Luke's resurrection narrative is organized around two primary episodes that together make the theological argument the entire Gospel has been building toward. The first is the empty tomb, where the women receive the announcement from two men in dazzling white — not one young man in white as in Mark — and carry the news to the eleven, who dismiss it as an idle tale. The second is the road to Emmaus, which is unique to Luke and which constitutes the most sustained post-resurrection narrative in any of the Gospels: two disciples walking away from Jerusalem, their hopes extinguished, joined by a stranger who opens the

Scriptures to them along the way and is recognized in the breaking of the bread.

The Emmaus narrative is the resurrection account that Luke lingers over, and the lingering is deliberate. The two disciples represent the condition of every subsequent reader who has encountered the events of the passion and found that the Jesus they thought they knew did not match the outcome that the cross produced. The stranger's question — was it not necessary that the Messiah should suffer these things and enter into his glory? — is the question the entire Gospel has been pressing toward. The necessity is not fate but theological logic: the one who proclaimed good news to the poor and release to the captives could not accomplish the deepest version of that release from a position of safety. The cross is where the pattern of the ministry reaches its fullest and most costly expression, and the resurrection is the confirmation that the pattern was right.

The recognition in the breaking of the bread is the culmination of Luke's sustained attention to meals as the space where the kingdom becomes visible. Jesus has eaten with Pharisees, with sinners, with tax collectors, with his disciples. He has told parables about feasts and banquets and the kinds of people who get invited to them. He has instituted the meal of remembrance in the upper room. And now the risen Jesus is recognized not in a vision, not in an audible declaration, not in the display of wounds, but in the familiar gesture of a guest who takes bread and blesses it and breaks it and gives it — the same gesture at Emmaus as at the feeding of the five thousand, the same gesture as at the Last Supper. The community that gathers around this table is the community Luke has been describing across twenty-four chapters: the community of those who were not looking for what they found and who recognized him in the moment of reception.

The Meaning of the Whole

Reading Luke's narrative from beginning to end — attending to the way the infancy narrative establishes theological stakes that the passion narrative fulfills, the way the travel narrative accumulates its argument about discipleship in the long middle of the story, the way the paired episodes and unique parables press their specific dimensions of the gospel's claim, the way the resurrection narratives interpret everything that preceded them — produces an understanding of the whole that is qualitatively different from anything achieved by engaging individual passages in isolation.

Luke is a carefully constructed argument about the scope of what God has done in Jesus and the range of people toward whom that action is directed. Its claim is that in this specific person, at this specific moment, the promise carried across the entire history of Israel has been fulfilled in a form that opens it to every person who has been excluded from its benefits by any of the social, economic, ethnic, or gender-based arrangements that human communities use to determine who belongs. The argument is not stated once and left at that. It is pressed from every angle across twenty-four chapters — in the songs of the infancy narrative, in the Nazareth announcement, in every meal Jesus attends and every boundary he crosses and every person he stops for who the culture has decided is not worth stopping for.

The Travel Narrative as Theological Architecture

One dimension of Luke's narrative structure that rewards closer attention is the deliberate use of the travel narrative not as a bridge between the Galilean ministry and the Jerusalem passion but as the Gospel's primary location for theological instruction. The journey framework does what no other structural device in the Synoptic tradition quite manages: it creates a sustained context in which the demands of discipleship can be developed at length, in encounter after encounter, without requiring the reader to imagine that Jesus has paused his ministry to deliver a lecture. The teaching happens on the road, in homes, around tables, in the middle of travel — which is itself a claim about where discipleship is formed.

The travel narrative is also the section where Luke's unique material is most concentrated, and the concentration reveals the specific concerns that distinguish Luke's theological agenda from the parallel accounts. The parables found only here — the Good Samaritan, the Prodigal Son, the Rich Man and Lazarus, the Pharisee and the Tax Collector — together constitute Luke's most sustained engagement with the questions of who is included in the kingdom's scope, what the economic implications of the kingdom's arrival are, and what prayer looks like when it is honest rather than performed. Each parable addresses a dimension of the gospel's claim that the surrounding narrative has been building toward and that the subsequent narrative will press further. Reading the travel narrative as a sequence of memorable but essentially independent stories misses the cumulative argument that only the sequence can carry. The journey moves toward Jerusalem, but it also moves toward the reader — pressing its demands closer and closer until there is no comfortable distance left from which to appreciate it without being required to respond.

Chapter 5

Key Themes

"The Spirit of the Lord is on me, because he has anointed me to proclaim good news to the poor. He has sent me to proclaim freedom for the prisoners and recovery of sight for the blind, to set the oppressed free, to proclaim the year of the Lord's favor."
— Luke 4:18-19

The Holy Spirit

No theme runs more consistently through Luke's Gospel than the presence and activity of the Holy Spirit. From the first chapter, where the Spirit fills John the Baptist in his mother's womb and overshadows Mary at the annunciation, to the final chapter, where the risen Jesus promises that the disciples will be clothed with power from on high, the Spirit is the active agent of the gospel's movement at every stage. Elizabeth is filled with the Spirit when she greets Mary. Zechariah is filled with the Spirit when he prophesies. Simeon is guided by the Spirit to the Temple at precisely the moment the infant Jesus arrives. The Spirit descends on Jesus at his baptism. The Spirit leads Jesus into the wilderness. Jesus returns to Galilee in the power of the Spirit and opens his Nazareth sermon with the declaration that the Spirit of the Lord is upon him.

This concentration of Spirit-language in Luke is not decorative. It is a sustained theological claim about the source and character of everything that happens in the Gospel. The Spirit in Luke is not a theological category applied to moments of unusual religious intensity. It is the active presence of God moving the story forward, enabling the proclamation, empowering the healings, guiding the encounters, and sustaining the community that will carry the gospel beyond the borders of Israel after the ascension. The same Spirit that fills the characters of the infancy narrative, that descends on Jesus at the Jordan, and that empowers the Galilean ministry will be poured out at Pentecost in Acts, and Luke places the promise of that pouring at the end of the Gospel so that the reader understands from the beginning of Acts that the continuation of the story is the Spirit's continuation.

The Spirit in Luke is also specifically the Spirit of joy. When Elizabeth is filled with the Spirit, she blesses Mary with a cry of joy. When Mary responds, she sings a song that is among the most joyful declarations in the Hebrew tradition. When Jesus rejoices in the Holy Spirit in chapter ten, it is in response to the disciples' successful mission and to the revelation of the kingdom's things to those the world considers insignificant. The connection between the Spirit and joy in Luke is not incidental. It is the formal expression of the Gospel's deepest theological conviction: that what the Spirit is doing in the world through Jesus is genuinely good news, and that the appropriate human response to genuine good news is genuine joy.

Prayer

Luke's Gospel presents a Jesus who prays more consistently and more visibly than any other Gospel's Jesus, and the pattern is so persistent and so precisely placed that it constitutes a structural argument about the nature of the mission Jesus carries. Jesus prays at his baptism, and it is while he is praying that the heaven opens and the Spirit descends. He withdraws to desolate places to pray during the Galilean ministry. He prays before choosing the twelve apostles. He is praying at the transfiguration, and it is while he is praying that his appearance is transformed. He prays in Gethsemane. He prays from the cross. The pattern is not random. Prayer precedes every major turning point in the narrative, and its consistent placement communicates a consistent claim: the mission Jesus carries is not self-generated. It is received, renewed, and sustained in the relationship between the Son and the Father that prayer both expresses and deepens.

Luke is also the Gospel that records the most teaching about prayer. The Lord's Prayer appears here, taught in response to a disciple's specific request — Lord, teach us to pray. The parable of the friend at midnight follows immediately and presses the community toward persistence: ask, seek, knock, and the heavenly Father will give the Holy Spirit to those who ask. The parable of the persistent widow in chapter eighteen — a woman whose relentless pursuit of justice from an unjust judge finally secures what she needs — is explicitly introduced as a parable about the need to pray always and not give up. The parable of the Pharisee and the tax collector turns on the question of what prayer looks like when it is honest rather than performed, and its verdict is unambiguous: the one who brings nothing to justify himself leaves justified, and the one who brings his own record leaves with nothing more than he arrived with.

For Luke's communities, navigating the extended present between resurrection and return, the teaching on prayer is not supplementary instruction for the spiritually inclined. It is the fundamental orientation of a community whose circumstances do not always confirm the goodness of what it believes. Prayer in Luke is not the expression of a relationship that is going well. It is the practice that sustains relationship through circumstances that press against it — the persistent widow's insistence on justice from a source whose responsiveness she cannot guarantee, the disciples' continuing request to an unseen Father in the middle of conditions that do not always feel like the kingdom's favor. The community that Luke is writing for needs this teaching not as inspiration but as instruction, and Luke places it at the center of the travel narrative where the instruction about discipleship in the long middle of the story is most concentrated.

Joy

Joy in Luke is not a mood. It is a theological category — the appropriate human response to the arrival of something that genuinely warrants it, pressed against circumstances that do not always confirm its grounds. The note is sounded in the first chapter and sustained across the entire Gospel. The angel announces great joy that will be for all people. The shepherds return glorifying and praising God. Simeon blesses God and is ready to depart in peace. The disciples return from their mission with joy. The father of the prodigal son celebrates with music and dancing. The woman who finds her lost coin calls her neighbors together to rejoice. In the final chapter, the disciples return to Jerusalem with great joy after the ascension, and they are continually in the Temple blessing God.

The joy Luke describes is consistently disproportionate — larger than the occasion seems to warrant by the standards of the surrounding culture's calculations about what constitutes a cause for celebration. The shepherd who finds one lost sheep leaves the ninety-nine and throws a party. The woman who finds one lost coin calls all her neighbors. The father who receives his returning prodigal kills the fattened calf and organizes a feast. In each case, the joy exceeds what observers think the situation warrants, and in each case, Luke presents the excess as the accurate response rather than the disproportionate one. The elder brother who stands outside the feast and tallies the cost of his father's generosity is not the one whose emotional register is calibrated to reality. He is the one whose sense of proportion has been formed by a framework that the kingdom has not yet reorganized.

The Poor and Economic Reversal

Luke's sustained attention to poverty, wealth, and the social effects of economic inequality constitutes one of the most distinctive and most demanding features of the entire Gospel. Jesus announces good news to the poor in the Nazareth synagogue, and the announcement is not a metaphor. The poor who appear in Luke's narrative are people whose material circumstances define their access to everything that makes human life possible — food, shelter, legal protection, social belonging, religious participation. The good news addressed to them is good news about those circumstances, not merely good news about their spiritual condition independently of those circumstances.

The Beatitudes in Luke differ significantly from Matthew's. Where Matthew's version reads blessed are the poor in spirit, Luke's reads blessed are you who are poor — a second-person declaration addressed to actual poor people, without the qualifying phrase that moves the focus from material to spiritual condition. The corresponding woes — woe to you who are rich, woe to you who are well fed now, woe to you who laugh now — are equally direct. Luke is not softening the economic edge of Jesus' proclamation. He is sharpening it, because the communities for whom he writes include both the poor who need to hear they are blessed and the wealthy who need to hear they are warned.

The parables unique to Luke press this theme from every available angle. The rich fool who builds bigger barns to store his surplus and dies before he can enjoy it is a portrait of a life organized around the wrong center. The rich man who feasts sumptuously while Lazarus lies at his gate dying is a portrait of the moral catastrophe that economic comfort produces when it is insulated from the visibility of suffering. Zacchaeus, the wealthy tax collector who climbs a tree to see Jesus and comes down to give half his possessions to the poor and restore fourfold what he has taken, is the portrait of what genuine encounter with Jesus produces in the life of a wealthy person who allows the encounter to reorganize his relationship to his wealth. The economic theme in Luke is not a single proposition applied repeatedly. It is a many-angled argument pressed with sustained seriousness across the entire Gospel.

Women and the Marginalized

Luke's Gospel presents a consistent and deliberate pattern of attention to people whom the surrounding world had placed at the margins of religious and social life. Women appear throughout the narrative with a frequency and theological agency unprecedented in ancient religious literature. The marginalized appear not as background context but as the primary subjects of the gospel's address. The pattern is theological before it is sociological: the kingdom that Jesus announces moves toward the margins as a matter of its own internal logic, not as a secondary application of principles established at the center.

The women in Luke are named, active, and theologically significant at every stage of the narrative. Mary receives the annunciation and responds with a theological declaration that shapes the Gospel's understanding of reversal and faithful receptivity. Elizabeth confirms the divine initiative and praises the one who believed. Anna the prophetess speaks about the child to all who are waiting for redemption. The women who travel with Jesus and support his ministry from their own resources are doing something the surrounding culture did not provide a ready category for, and Luke names them explicitly and publicly. The women at the cross remain when the male disciples have gone. The women at the tomb are the first witnesses of the resurrection. The pattern across the entire Gospel is consistent: women are present at the most theologically significant moments of the narrative, and their presence is not incidental background.

The marginalized more broadly — the lepers, the blind beggars, the tax collectors, the sinners, the Samaritans, the Gentile centurion, the dying criminal — appear throughout Luke's narrative as the people toward whom Jesus moves with a consistency that becomes its own argument about the character of the God he represents. The leper who returns to give thanks is a Samaritan. The model of neighborly love in the most famous parable is a Samaritan. The faith Jesus commends as exceeding what he has found in Israel belongs to a Roman officer. These are not isolated surprise reversals scattered through an otherwise conventional narrative. They are the concentrated expression of a sustained theological claim that the kingdom's scope has always exceeded the boundaries that any human community has drawn around it.

Repentance and Forgiveness

No theme is more consistently and more joyfully developed in Luke than the theme of repentance and the forgiveness it receives. The three parables of chapter fifteen are the most sustained exploration of this theme in the entire Gospel, but the exploration runs from John the Baptist's opening proclamation through the risen Jesus' final commission to proclaim repentance and forgiveness of sins to all nations. Repentance in Luke is not primarily a condition that must be met before forgiveness becomes available. It is the human movement toward a forgiveness that has already been initiated by the one who goes looking for the lost before they have begun looking for home.

The parable of the prodigal son is the most complete portrait of repentance in Luke. The son comes to himself in the far country, rehearses a speech of self-presentation as a hired servant rather than a son, and begins the long walk home. But the father sees him while he is still a long way off and runs to meet him, and the embrace and the robe and the ring arrive before the speech has been delivered. The repentance that the son intended to perform has been overtaken by a reception he did not imagine he was eligible for. This sequence — the movement toward home met by a movement from home that is faster and more generous

— is the shape of the forgiveness Luke presents as the content of the good news. The repentance is real and necessary. The forgiveness is not its reward. It is the reality toward which the repentance is moving and which was already moving toward the repentance before the repentance began.

The Kingdom of God

The kingdom of God in Luke carries the same central significance it carries in the other Gospels, but Luke's treatment of it has a distinctive temporal quality that reflects his community's situation. The kingdom is present in the ministry of Jesus — when the Pharisees ask when the kingdom of God is coming, Jesus tells them it is already in their midst. But the kingdom is also future — the disciples are taught to pray for its coming, and the travel narrative is organized around the journey toward the city where the cross will both reveal and advance its arrival. And the kingdom is the horizon of the extended present — the period between resurrection and return in which the community must live faithfully without the visible confirmation that full arrival would provide.

Luke's handling of this temporal complexity is one of his most significant theological contributions. He does not resolve the tension between the kingdom's present reality and its future completeness by collapsing one into the other. The kingdom is genuinely present in the healings, the exorcisms, the forgiveness, the table fellowship, the restoration of the excluded. It is also genuinely future in its full scope and final form. And the community that lives between these two realities is the community that the travel narrative's teaching on discipleship is addressed to — the community that must organize its life around a center whose full vindication it has not yet seen and that the surrounding world has not yet been compelled to acknowledge.

Meals and Table Fellowship

Luke's Gospel records more meals than any other, and its sustained attention to who eats with whom, and under what conditions, constitutes one of its most distinctive theological arguments. Meals in the ancient Mediterranean world were among the most socially structured contexts of daily life: who reclined at the table and in what position communicated information about hierarchy, belonging, and relationship that everyone present could read. Jesus' table fellowship in Luke consistently violates the social logic that organizes these arrangements, and the violations are not accidental. They are the enacted form of the kingdom's claim about who belongs in the presence of God.

Jesus eats with Pharisees and with tax collectors. He attends a banquet where a sinful woman anoints his feet and defends her action against the host's unspoken objection. He tells a parable about a great banquet whose originally invited guests all decline, producing an invitation extended to the poor, the crippled, the blind, and the lame — and then to people on the roads and in the lanes outside the city, because there is still room and the host intends the house to be full. The Zacchaeus episode ends with Jesus announcing that he must stay at this man's house — a declaration of table fellowship that the crowd regards as the most scandalous choice Jesus could have made, and that Luke presents as the precise expression of the Son of Man's mission to seek and save the lost. The risen Jesus is recognized at Emmaus in the breaking of the bread. The meal is where the kingdom becomes visible in Luke, and the question of who is at the table is always also the question of who the kingdom includes.

The Death That Interprets Everything

As in Mark, the death of Jesus in Luke is not an appendix to the story but the destination toward which the entire narrative has been moving. But Luke's theological framing of the cross is distinctive. Where Mark allows the cry of dereliction to stand in its full darkness, Luke presents a Jesus who maintains to the end the character of the ministry he has conducted throughout: praying for those who crucify him, promising paradise to the criminal who asks only to be remembered, commending his spirit into his Father's hands with a word of trust rather than abandonment. The cross in Luke is the costliest expression of everything that has been true of Jesus from the Nazareth synagogue onward — the same movement toward the excluded, the same forgiveness extended before it has been earned, the same prayer sustaining a mission that the surrounding world regards as defeated.

The necessity of the cross is stated most clearly in the Emmaus narrative, where the risen Jesus asks his unrecognizing companions whether it was not necessary that the Messiah should suffer these things and enter into his glory. The necessity is not external fate but internal logic: the one who came to seek and save the lost could not accomplish the deepest version of that saving from a position of safety. The cross is where the pattern of the ministry — good news to the poor, release to the captives, freedom for the oppressed — meets its most extreme and most comprehensive expression. The death that interprets everything in Luke is not the dark center around which the rest must be arranged. It is the furthest reach of the same movement that began in Nazareth when Jesus read from Isaiah and announced that the Scripture was fulfilled in their hearing.

Chapter 6

Where People Get It Wrong

"Blessed are you who are poor, for yours is the kingdom of God."
— Luke 6:20

Reading Luke as the Sentimental Gospel

The most pervasive misreading of Luke treats it as the Gospel of warmth and welcome — the accessible one, the one with the best stories, the one whose Jesus is most reliably gentle and most reliably approachable. On this reading, Luke is the Gospel you recommend to people who find Mark too urgent and Matthew too demanding and John too cosmic. Its portrait of Jesus eating with sinners, welcoming children, stopping for the sick and the poor and the excluded, is received as an invitation to feel good about a God who is fundamentally accepting, and the parables of chapter fifteen are read as confirmation that this acceptance is unconditional and costs nothing in the receiving.

This reading captures something real and misses everything important. Luke is the most demanding Gospel on the specific questions of wealth, economic practice, and the reorganization of social relationships that genuine reception of the kingdom requires. Its Jesus does not simply welcome the excluded. He announces a reorganization of the social order that places the currently powerful at genuine risk and requires the currently comfortable to make choices that their comfort actively resists. The Beatitudes in Luke come with corresponding woes. The rich man who ignores Lazarus does not end up in a place of gentle correction. The elder brother who resents his father's generosity is left outside the feast at the end of the parable, and the question of whether he will enter is not answered within the narrative. Luke is warm where warmth is the gospel's appropriate form. It is searching and uncomfortable where the gospel's demands require honesty rather than reassurance.

Spiritualizing the Beatitudes

The difference between Luke's Beatitudes and Matthew's is one of the most consequential textual variations in the Gospels, and the direction of misreading almost always runs the same way: Luke's version is read through Matthew's, and the material specificity of Luke's version is quietly dissolved into the spiritual interiority of Matthew's. Blessed are you who are poor becomes blessed are the poor in spirit. Woe to you who are rich disappears entirely from the interpretive framework, because the woes have no parallel in Matthew and their absence there makes them easier to overlook or spiritualize in Luke.

The misreading matters because the communities Luke was writing for included actual poor people whose material circumstances were the direct subject of the declaration, and actual wealthy people whose relationship to their wealth was the direct subject of the warning. Spiritualizing the Beatitudes does not merely soften a difficult text. It inverts its direction: instead of an announcement to the materially poor that the kingdom is genuinely theirs, it becomes an announcement to the spiritually humble that God approves of their interior disposition — a reading that applies equally to the wealthy and the poor and therefore makes no particular demand on either. The woes disappear into irrelevance because the spiritual reading has no mechanism by which material prosperity becomes a spiritual warning. Luke did not write the woes by accident, and reading them out of the text by importing Matthew's framework is a misreading with direct and specific consequences for how communities of faith understand their relationship to economic life.

Flattening the Parables into Morality Tales

Luke's parables are among the most familiar passages in all of Scripture, and familiarity is one of the most reliable producers of misreading. The Good Samaritan is regularly read as a general lesson about kindness to strangers. The Prodigal Son is read as a general lesson about forgiveness and second chances. The Pharisee and the Tax Collector is read as a general lesson about humility in prayer. Each of these readings captures something present in the text and misses the specific, targeted, culturally embedded argument the parable is making that the general moral lesson cannot carry.

The Good Samaritan is not a general lesson about neighborliness. It is a specific and deliberate provocation addressed to a Torah expert who has asked what he must do to inherit eternal life and then, when Jesus has affirmed the great commandment, asked the follow-up question that reveals his real concern: who is my neighbor? The parable answers this question by placing a Samaritan — a figure the Torah expert's tradition regarded as an ethnic and religious outsider with whom faithful Jews minimized contact — in the position of the one who fulfills the love commandment. The parable does not merely illustrate the principle that neighborly love crosses social boundaries. It forces the Torah expert to say aloud that the one who showed mercy was the Samaritan, and then to receive the command to go and do likewise. The discomfort the parable creates is not incidental to its meaning. It is its meaning, pressed to the precise point where the hearer must either receive it or refuse it.

The Prodigal Son is similarly misread when it is treated as a story primarily about the younger son's repentance and return. As Chapter 4 noted, the parable contains three characters, and the third — the elder brother who stands outside the feast — is the one whose response is left unresolved at the end of the narrative. The parable is addressed to Pharisees and scribes who are grumbling about Jesus' welcome of tax collectors and sinners, and the elder brother's position outside the feast corresponds precisely to theirs. The question the parable presses is not whether the father will receive the returning prodigal. That question is answered immediately and extravagantly. The question it leaves open is whether the elder brother will enter the feast — whether the people who have been faithful within the existing religious framework will be able to receive a generosity that their framework has not prepared them for and that their own careful record of faithfulness has not earned them any advantage in receiving.

Misunderstanding Luke's Universalism as Cheap Inclusivity

Luke's sustained concern with Gentile inclusion and the scope of the gospel's reach has sometimes generated a misreading that treats it as a general principle of divine acceptance that dissolves all distinctions and makes no demands. On this reading, the God of Luke is simply inclusive — welcoming everyone regardless of background, requiring nothing that would distinguish the life of those who receive the gospel from the life of those who do not. The universalism becomes a form of theological pluralism in which the specific claims of the gospel are softened into a general affirmation that God loves everyone and that love requires nothing in particular in response.

This misreading inverts Luke's actual argument. The universalism of Luke's Gospel is not the erasure of particularity but the extension of a particular claim to its full scope. The God who acts in Jesus is the God of Israel, whose covenant with Abraham always carried the promise that all nations would be blessed through his descendants. The fulfillment of that promise does not dissolve the specificity of the claim. It presses it outward until it reaches the people who were always its intended beneficiaries. The Gentile centurion whose servant Jesus heals is not welcomed because his beliefs are irrelevant. He is commended because his faith — in the specific person standing before him, with the specific authority Jesus has demonstrated — is genuine and complete. The universal scope of the gospel in Luke is the scope of a specific claim about a specific person, extended without remainder to every person who will receive it. It is the opposite of the undifferentiated acceptance that the misreading assumes.

Collapsing Luke into Acts

Because Luke wrote both the Gospel and Acts as a two-volume work addressed to the same recipient, there is a persistent temptation to read the two as interchangeable parts of a single continuous narrative — to import the theology of Acts back into the Gospel or to read the Gospel primarily as a prologue to the real story that begins at Pentecost. Both directions of this collapse produce misreadings. Reading Acts back into Luke makes the Gospel's ending feel like a pause rather than a conclusion, and imports the developed ecclesiology of Acts into a narrative that has not yet reached the events that make it possible. Reading Luke primarily as a prologue to Acts diminishes the theological significance of the Gospel's own structure and argument, treating the infancy narrative, the travel narrative, and the resurrection appearances as setup rather than substance.

The two volumes are genuinely continuous and genuinely distinct. The Gospel is complete in itself: it moves from Temple to Temple, from the announcement of John's birth to the disciples' return to Jerusalem with great joy, and its argument about who Jesus is and what his coming means does not require Acts to complete it. Acts is the extension of the Gospel's argument into new territory — the movement of the same gospel, empowered by the same Spirit, toward the ends of the earth that the Gospel's final commission announces but does not narrate. Reading the two well requires holding their continuity and their distinctness simultaneously, allowing each to illuminate the other without allowing either to be absorbed into the other.

Treating the Travel Narrative as Filler

The travel narrative of chapters nine through nineteen is the section of Luke most consistently underread by readers who are familiar with Luke's most famous passages. Because it lacks the obvious dramatic momentum of the Galilean ministry and the passion narrative, and because its geographical progress toward Jerusalem is so loosely tracked that readers sometimes lose the sense that a journey is actually occurring, it is often treated as a collection of miscellaneous material that Luke has organized into a journey framework for convenience rather than for theological purpose. Individual passages are extracted and read in isolation — the Good Samaritan, the Prodigal Son, Zacchaeus — while the section as a whole is not read as the sustained argument about discipleship in the extended present that Chapter 4 described.

The misreading has direct consequences for how Luke's teaching on prayer, wealth, and social relationships is received. These themes are developed with their greatest concentration and their most sustained pressure in the travel narrative, and reading individual passages without attending to the section's cumulative argument produces a thinner engagement with each passage than the section's architecture is designed to produce. The parable of the persistent widow makes a different kind of sense when it is read as part of a sustained section of teaching about prayer that includes the Lord's Prayer, the friend at midnight, and the Pharisee and the tax collector. The Zacchaeus episode carries different weight when it is read as the culmination of a travel narrative that has been pressing the economic demands of discipleship across ten chapters. The travel narrative is not filler. It is Luke's primary location for the teaching that the community most needs in the long middle of the story, and reading it well requires reading it as a whole.

Reading the Prodigal Son as Primarily about the Younger Son

The most common misreading of Luke's most famous parable focuses the entire interpretive weight on the younger son's journey — his departure, his degradation, his coming to himself, his return, his reception. This is not an unreasonable reading of a significant portion of the parable's content. But it misses the deliberate structural decision Luke has made in ending the parable where he does and with whom he does. The elder brother's refusal to enter the feast, and the father's patient pleading with him outside the door, are not a secondary subplot appended to the main story. They are the hinge on which the parable's primary argument turns.

The parable is addressed to Pharisees and scribes who are grumbling that Jesus receives sinners and eats with them. The younger son corresponds to the sinners Jesus is receiving. The elder brother corresponds to the Pharisees and scribes who are grumbling about the reception. The father corresponds to the God whose character the entire parable is designed to reveal. The question the parable is pressing toward its actual audience — the grumblers outside the feast — is whether they will enter. The father's speech to the elder brother is addressed to them as directly as anything in the Gospel: son, you are always with me, and everything I have is yours, but we had to celebrate and be glad, because this brother of yours was dead and is alive again. The parable does not tell us whether the elder brother entered. It does not tell us whether the Pharisees and scribes received what

Jesus was telling them. It leaves the question open, pressing it toward every subsequent reader who has ever found themselves outside a generosity they cannot quite bring themselves to celebrate.

Misreading Luke's Economic Demands as Optional Application

A final and pervasive misreading of Luke treats its economic teaching as one application among many of general spiritual principles — an emphasis that may be particularly relevant for some readers in some circumstances but that does not constitute a universal demand binding on all who receive the gospel. The rich man who builds bigger barns becomes a warning against materialism in the abstract. The rich man and Lazarus becomes a story about the importance of compassion. Zacchaeus becomes an encouraging example of generosity. The economic edge of each text is acknowledged and then softened into a general spiritual principle that makes no specific demand on the reader's actual financial life.

This reading is available to anyone willing to maintain sufficient distance from the texts while engaging them, and Luke's Gospel consistently refuses to make that distance comfortable. The rich ruler who comes to Jesus asking what he must do to inherit eternal life and goes away sorrowful because he has great possessions is presented without softening: Jesus watches him go, observes that it is hard for the wealthy to enter the kingdom of God, and does not call him back to negotiate. The disciples are astonished, and Jesus' response — with man this is impossible, but with God all things are possible — does not diminish the demand. It relocates the resource for meeting it. The economic teaching of Luke is not a spiritual metaphor for the importance of holding things loosely. It is a concrete demand about actual financial life, pressed with the same specificity that the Beatitudes' woes and the parable of the rich man and Lazarus press it, and receiving it as anything less than that is a domestication that Luke's own narrative does not permit.

Chapter 7

What It Means for Modern Life

"For the Son of Man came to seek and to save the lost."
— Luke 19:10

Living Faithfully in the Long Middle

The most fundamental practical implication of Luke for modern readers is the one the travel narrative never stops pressing: the kingdom of God has arrived, its full completion has not, and the community of faith must organize its life faithfully in the extended present between those two realities without collapsing them into each other. This is the situation Luke's original communities were navigating, and it is the situation every generation of the church has inhabited since. The temptation runs in two directions simultaneously: to treat the kingdom's presence as so complete that the cross's demands no longer apply, or to treat its future completion as so distant that the present requires nothing more than patient waiting. Luke refuses both. The travel narrative exists precisely to describe what faithful life in the long middle actually looks like — not in general but in the specific texture of daily choices about money, prayer, social belonging, and the direction in which one's attention and resources consistently move.

Living in the long middle means, practically, that the standards of discipleship Luke commends in the travel narrative are not ideals reserved for a future state of spiritual maturity. They are the description of a life genuinely organized around the kingdom's values in circumstances that the kingdom has not yet fully transformed. The person who takes Luke's call seriously will find it pressing on precisely the points where the surrounding culture — which tends to organize life around the accumulation of security, the management of social reputation, and the protection of existing advantage — pushes consistently in the opposite direction. The first and most foundational feature of life shaped by Luke's call is this: it is organized around the movement the Gospel consistently commends, which is the movement toward the excluded rather than the movement toward those who can reciprocate.

This movement is not passive or sentimental. Luke's Jesus is the most consistently active figure in the Gospel — constantly in motion, constantly stopping for people the culture has decided are not worth stopping for, constantly pressing toward the city where the cost of the mission will reach its maximum. The call is not to withdrawal from the world's work but to engagement organized around different values and moving in a consistently different direction than the engagement the surrounding culture commends. When Jesus tells Zacchaeus that he must stay at his house today, the must is not compulsion. It is the natural expression of a mission that cannot be redirected toward more socially acceptable destinations. The life shaped by Luke's call has the same quality of directional consistency: it moves toward the Zacchaeuses, the Lazaruses at the gate, the women who have been excluded from full participation in religious and public life, not because they are sentimental favorites but because that is the direction in which the kingdom consistently moves.

The Practical Reordering of Wealth

The implications of Luke's economic teaching for modern life are more specific and more demanding than most readings acknowledge. Luke does not offer a general principle of generosity that each reader applies according to their own judgment about what generosity requires in their particular circumstances. It offers a sustained, many-angled argument that the organization of one's financial life around the accumulation and protection of personal advantage is incompatible with the organization of one's life around the kingdom — and that the incompatibility is not a tension to be managed but a choice to be made.

The rich man who builds bigger barns is not condemned for building barns. He is condemned for the conclusion he draws from their fullness: that his life is now secured for many years and he can eat, drink, and be merry. The problem is not prosperity but the relationship between prosperity and security — the assumption that what he has accumulated is sufficient to organize a life around, that the soul can be satisfied by what the barns contain. The question God asks him — this night your soul is required of you, and the things you have prepared, whose will they be? — is not a threat. It is an honest description of the situation he has misread. He has organized his life around something that cannot bear the weight he has placed on it, and the night reveals the misplaced center that the fullness of the barns had obscured.

The practical application of this teaching requires more than deciding to give more money to worthy causes while leaving the fundamental orientation of one's financial life unchanged. It requires the honest examination that Luke's parables consistently press: what is the soul actually organized around? What does the pattern of one's financial choices reveal about where genuine security is being sought and what is being held in reserve against the demands the kingdom might make? Zacchaeus does not give a percentage. He gives half his possessions to the poor and restores fourfold what he has taken — a response so disproportionate to what was asked that it communicates something about the interior reorganization that the encounter with Jesus has produced. The economic teaching of Luke is not a call to imprudent generosity but a call to honest examination of the relationship between one's financial life and the actual center of gravity around which one's existence is organized.

The Cost of Genuine Inclusion

Luke's sustained attention to the excluded carries direct implications for modern communities of faith that are more specific and more demanding than a general commitment to welcome can absorb. The pattern Luke describes is not a pattern of being open to people who present themselves at the door. It is a pattern of going to where the excluded are, stopping for them in ways that cost social capital, eating with them in ways that disturb the observers, and defending the practice against the objections of people who have their own framework for determining who belongs in religious community and find that Jesus consistently violates it.

The practical question Luke presses on modern communities is not whether they are welcoming in principle but whether their actual practice of community life reproduces the pattern of Jesus' ministry or the pattern of the surrounding culture's social arrangements. Every community of faith organizes its attention around some people more than others, makes some people feel immediately at home and leaves others uncertain whether the welcome announced from the front extends to them specifically. The communities that have genuinely received Luke's argument are the communities whose actual practice — not their stated values but their observable pattern of attention, resource allocation, and the direction in which their most significant relationships move — corresponds to the directional consistency of Jesus' ministry. These communities are not uncommon. They are also not the norm, and the gap between stated welcome and actual practice is one of the most consistent sources of the credibility deficit that communities of faith in the contemporary world are navigating.

The social cost of genuine inclusion in Luke is not merely the cost of accepting people who are different. It is the cost of the social reconfiguration that genuine inclusion requires — the reorganization of who sits where at the table, who has standing in the community's internal life, whose voice carries weight in the decisions that determine what the community values and how it spends its resources. The Pharisee who invites Jesus to dinner and watches the sinful woman anoint his feet is not simply failing to welcome a guest. He is confronting the specific implication of Jesus' presence in his home: that the woman he has categorized as a sinner has received a forgiveness, he has not recognized his own need for, and that her presence at the table is the direct consequence of the character of the one he has invited. Genuine inclusion in Luke is not the management of social diversity. It is the consequence of receiving the one who has already moved toward the excluded, and whose movement consistently reorganizes the social arrangements of every community he enters.

Failure and the Running Father

One of Luke's most immediately relevant contributions to modern life is its honest and joyful portrayal of restoration after failure — not the restoration of institutional credibility through subsequent performance but the restoration of relationship by the specific, running, ahead-of-the-speech generosity of the one who has been failed. The parable of the prodigal son is the most concentrated expression of this in the Gospel, but the pattern runs throughout Luke: the sinful woman is forgiven before she has made any articulate request, only after she has expressed what she could express through tears and perfume and the unbinding of her hair. Zacchaeus is received before he has announced his decision to give half his possessions. The criminal on the cross is promised paradise before he has had time to demonstrate anything about the sincerity of his request.

For modern communities of faith that know their own patterns of failure — their tendency to organize around the wrong centers, their capacity for the elder brother's resentment, their institutional instinct to manage the credibility consequences of failure rather than receive the restoration that addresses it — this pattern is among Luke's most sustaining contributions. The comfort is genuine: the father runs. The distance between the returning prodigal and the embrace he receives is the distance the father covers before the son has finished his approach, and the speech the son has prepared is interrupted by the robe and the ring and the invitation to the feast. This is the shape of the restoration that Luke presents as the gospel's content. It is not earned by the quality of the repentance. It is the reality toward which the repentance is moving, already in motion before the repentance has completed its approach.

The demand the pattern makes is equally genuine: the restoration Luke describes requires the willingness to receive it rather than performing a recovery that bypasses it. The prodigal who returns rehearsing his speech of self-presentation as a hired servant is not wrong to rehearse it. He is simply overtaken by something more generous than the arrangement he was prepared to negotiate. The community that has experienced its own version of the prodigal's departure — its own ways of taking what it was given and spending it in ways that do not correspond to the character of the one who gave it — is invited to the same reception. Not to earn its way back through subsequent faithfulness, though faithfulness will follow. But to receive the embrace and the robe and the feast that are already being prepared and that do not wait for the speech to be completed before they begin.

Prayer in an Anxious Age

Luke's teaching on prayer has more immediate relevance to the contemporary moment than any summary of its content can convey. The specific form of anxiety that Luke's parables on prayer address is not the anxiety of people whose material needs

are unmet. It is the anxiety of people in the middle of the story —
people who know what they believe, who are trying to live
accordingly, and who find that the gap between the kingdom's
announced presence and the conditions of daily life does not
always confirm the goodness of what they believe. The persistent
widow is not doubting the existence of the judge. She is pressing
him for what the relationship between them requires him to
provide, in circumstances that do not yet reflect the justice she is
claiming.

This is the situation of every community of faith that prays
for the coming of the kingdom in circumstances where the
kingdom's full arrival is not yet evident. Luke does not address
this situation by minimizing the gap between the kingdom's
announced presence and the conditions that press against it. He
addresses it by commending the posture of the persistent widow:
the continued, specific, unembarrassed pressing of the claim on
the one who is able to answer it, without the resignation that treats
the gap as evidence that the claim was mistaken. The parable's
conclusion — will not God bring about justice for his chosen
ones who cry out to him day and night? — is a rhetorical question
that Luke places in Jesus' mouth as a direct challenge to the
community's willingness to maintain the posture the widow
represents through circumstances that make maintaining it costly.

For communities living in an era documented as one of the
most anxious in recorded history — where the management of
anxiety has become a significant industry and where the gap
between material comfort and genuine wellbeing is among the
most discussed features of contemporary life — Luke's teaching
on prayer offers a resource that is neither a therapeutic technique
nor a spiritual exercise in the general sense. It is the specific,
concrete, relationally grounded practice of pressing the claim of
the kingdom on the one who has made the claim, in the company
of a community that does the same, in the confidence that the one

who has promised is the one who runs toward the returning prodigal rather than waiting for the speech to be complete.

Joy as Resistance

Luke's consistent note of joy carries a quality that is easily missed when it is read as an emotional characteristic of the Gospel rather than a theological claim about the character of what God is doing in the world. The joy Luke commends is not the joy of comfortable circumstances or confirmed expectations. It is the joy that the shepherd feels when the lost sheep is found — disproportionate to what observers would calculate, but accurate to the reality of what has happened. It is the joy that the disciples bring back from their mission. It is the joy with which the disciples return to Jerusalem after the ascension, in full awareness of what the days preceding the ascension contained.

In a cultural moment characterized by pervasive anxiety, performative positivity that papers over genuine difficulty, and the kind of despair that arises when circumstances do not confirm the stories people have organized their lives around, Luke's joy is a form of resistance. Not resistance to honest engagement with what is genuinely difficult — Luke contains Gethsemane, the weeping over Jerusalem, the darkness of the cross. It is resistance to the conclusion that the difficulty is the final word, that what is lost is permanently lost, that the circumstances of the present moment determine the truth of what God is doing. The joy Luke commends is the joy of a community that knows the sheep has been found even when it is still looking for the way home, that knows the father is already running even before the prodigal has come into view, that knows the stone has been rolled away even while the journey to the tomb is still being made in grief.

The Table as Community Practice

Luke's sustained attention to meals as the space where the kingdom becomes visible has direct implications for how communities of faith understand the practice that most directly embodies that visibility in their own common life. The table in Luke is consistently the place where the social logic of the surrounding culture is reorganized by the presence of the one who hosts it — where the people who would not ordinarily eat together find themselves at the same meal, where the host's generosity is calibrated not by the social standing of the guests but by the character of the one whose presence transforms the occasion.

The practical implication is not primarily about the communion table, though it includes it. It is about the actual pattern of table fellowship that a community's life produces — about who eats with whom, in whose homes and under whose hospitality, whether the social arrangements of the surrounding culture determine who naturally gravitates toward whom within the community or whether something else is actively reorganizing those arrangements. The question Luke's sustained attention to meals presses on every community of faith is not whether the Lord's Supper is properly administered. It is whether the table practices of the community's common life correspond to the table practices of the Gospel it proclaims — whether the people who share the cup also share meals in ways that cross the social boundaries that organize the surrounding culture's social life.

Care for the Vulnerable as the Shape of the Mission

Luke's portrait of Jesus moving consistently toward the vulnerable — the lepers, the blind, the poor, the women whose social standing gave them no recognized claim on anyone's attention — describes not only what Jesus does but what the community that follows him is called to do. The care of the vulnerable in Luke is not a secondary application of the gospel to social needs. It is the primary form that the gospel's arrival takes when it is received by people who have understood what it claims. The Nazareth announcement is programmatic: good news to the poor, release to the captives, recovery of sight to the blind, freedom for the oppressed. These are not illustrations of the kingdom's arrival. They are its content, and the community that carries the gospel carries the responsibility for embodying that content in its own common life.

The parable of the great banquet makes this explicit in a way that the general principle of care for the vulnerable does not. When the originally invited guests all decline, the host's instruction to the servant is specific: go out quickly into the streets and alleys of the town and bring in the poor, the crippled, the blind, and the lame. And when there is still room, go out to the roads and country lanes and compel them to come in, so that my house will be full. The compulsion is not coercion but the insistence of a generosity that will not be satisfied with a partial filling of the seats. The house is meant to be full. The community that has received this parable as its description of the mission's scope will find that it cannot be satisfied with a welcome that extends only to the guests who present themselves without being sought.

The Cross and the Pattern of the Whole

The most profound and most demanding contribution Luke makes to modern life is the one that the Emmaus narrative states most directly: it was necessary that the Messiah should suffer these things and enter into his glory. The necessity is not external fate imposing itself on the story from outside. It is the internal logic of a mission whose character required the cross — because the one who came to seek and save the lost could not accomplish the deepest version of that saving from a position of safety, and because the pattern of the ministry was always moving in the direction the cross finally took to its limit.

The cross as the shape of Luke's Gospel for modern life means, practically, that the directional consistency of the ministry — toward the excluded, toward the vulnerable, toward the people from whom life has been taken — cannot be maintained without cost in a world organized around different values. The community that moves toward the margins will encounter the resistance that the surrounding culture mounts against anything that threatens its organization of advantage. The community that reorganizes its economic life around the kingdom's values will encounter the resistance of the frameworks that have organized financial life around accumulation and security. The community that extends the table's fellowship across the social boundaries that organize the surrounding culture's social life will encounter the resistance of the people who have invested in those boundaries and who experience their crossing as a threat.

Luke does not pretend that the cost of maintaining the mission's directional consistency is manageable. The cross is the evidence that it is not. But Luke also does not end at the cross. The risen Jesus who walks with the two disciples toward Emmaus, who opens the Scriptures to them and breaks the bread with them and is recognized in the breaking, is the confirmation that the pattern was right and the cost was worth paying. The community that has organized its life around the mission's directional consistency will find, as every generation before it has found, that the one who goes ahead toward Emmaus is genuinely there — and that the recognition that comes in the breaking of the bread is the joy that Luke has been pressing toward from the first chapter's songs to the final chapter's great joy. This is what Luke means for modern life. Not the comfort of a God who accepts everyone without requiring anything, but the demanding and sustaining reality of a God who runs toward the lost before they have finished returning, who sets a table for people who had no claim to an invitation, and who is recognized in the breaking of the bread by people who had stopped believing he was present.

Chapter 8

Modern Reflection

*"Were not our hearts burning within us while he talked with us on
the road and opened the Scriptures to us?"*
— Luke 24:32

Questions for Engagement with Luke's Gospel

The previous chapter examined what Luke makes possible for
modern readers — how its specific teachings on wealth, inclusion,
prayer, and the directional consistency of the mission can be
applied as practical resources for daily life and community. This
chapter is concerned with a different question: what Luke does to
the reader over time. Not the immediate application of a text to a
specific situation, but the slower, less visible formation that
happens when a person engages with the Gospel seriously and
repeatedly across different seasons of life, bringing each season's
specific experience to the text and allowing the text to press its
specific claims toward that experience. Luke is designed to be
revisited rather than completed. Its depth is not all visible on the
surface, and the formation it produces is the formation of
sustained encounter rather than the acquisition of content.

One of the most pressing questions facing modern culture is
whether genuine encounter is possible in a world shaped by the
management of impression and the curation of self-presentation.
Luke's Gospel addresses this question obliquely but persistently.
The encounters it describes are consistently unmanaged: the sinful
woman enters a Pharisee's dinner uninvited and breaks open an
alabaster jar. Zacchaeus climbs a tree and is addressed by name by
someone who has apparently already decided where he is eating

tonight. The two disciples on the road to Emmaus have a conversation with a stranger that reorganizes everything they thought they knew, without recognizing until the breaking of bread that the stranger was the risen Jesus. These are not encounters the participants arranged. They are encounters that arrive from outside the framework of expectation and produce responses that the framework could not have generated.

The Distinctive Character of Luke's Encounter

Luke's Gospel describes encounter with Jesus with an attentiveness to the interior experience of those who encounter him that is distinctive among the Gospels. The Emmaus disciples ask each other whether their hearts were not burning within them as he opened the Scriptures on the road. The sinful woman's tears and the extravagance of her gesture communicate something that she cannot say in the company of those present. Mary sits at Jesus' feet and chooses the better part in a way that Martha cannot understand from where she is standing. These interior dimensions of encounter are not psychological ornamentation. They are Luke's argument that the encounters the Gospel describes reach a level of the person that is deeper than behavioral response — that what Jesus produces in those who genuinely encounter him is a reorganization of the interior life that precedes and grounds whatever exterior change follows.

The physicality of Luke's encounter also matters for the formation of the reader. The father runs. The woman searches the house with a lamp until she finds the coin. The shepherd lifts the sheep onto his shoulders. Jesus stoops and writes in the dust. He takes the bread and blesses it and breaks it. These physical details are not incidental. They are constitutive of the portrait Luke is painting — a portrait in which the full embodied reality of the encounters the Gospel describes is as much a part of the theological claim as the teachings those encounters produce. The

God of Luke's Gospel is not primarily a principle or a framework. He is the father who runs and the shepherd who carries and the woman who searches, and the theological claims the Gospel makes about him cannot be separated from the specific physical gestures in which those claims are enacted.

The Parables as Mirror

The parables unique to Luke function over time as mirrors in which the reader encounters not only the character of the God they describe but their own character in response to that God. This is most concentrated in the parable of the prodigal son, where the three characters — the father, the younger son, and the elder brother — provide three positions from which the reader can locate their own experience. Most readers begin with the younger son's position: the one who has departed, who has squandered what was given, who needs the restoration the father provides. Over time, and with honest engagement, many readers recognize themselves in the elder brother — the one who has been faithful within the framework, who has accumulated a record of compliance, and who finds that a generosity extended to someone who has not earned it generates something in them that they would rather not name.

The formation that sustained engagement with the elder brother produces is among the most searching that Luke offers. It requires the reader to examine not only whether they have received the gospel's welcome but whether they have genuinely celebrated that welcome being extended to people whose reception costs them something — people whose presence at the table reorganizes a community in ways that make the long-faithful uncomfortable, people whose forgiveness requires those who have been less comprehensively wrong to receive them without the satisfaction of observed consequence. The elder brother is not outside the feast because the father has excluded him. He is outside because he cannot bring himself to enter on the terms that the feast requires. Every reader who has stood outside a generosity they could not quite celebrate has been where the elder brother is standing, and Luke leaves the question of whether he entered deliberately unresolved so that the reader must answer it for themselves.

The Failure of Managed Discipleship

The emergence of programmatic approaches to spiritual formation has produced a specific problem that Luke's Gospel addresses with unusual directness. The fundamental difficulty with managed discipleship in Luke's terms is not that programs are bad but that the formation the Gospel describes happens primarily through encounter and the reorganization that genuine encounter produces, not through the acquisition of content and the demonstration of competency. The disciples in Luke are not formed through curriculum. They are formed through the sustained experience of traveling with someone whose presence consistently reorganizes the frameworks through which they understand what matters and why.

The travel narrative is the most extended portrait of this formation process in the Gospel. Across ten chapters, the disciples accompany Jesus toward Jerusalem, watching him stop for people they would have passed, hearing him tell stories that put the wrong people in the position of exemplar, observing him eat with people whose company their social formation has taught them to avoid. The formation is not primarily cognitive. It is the slow recalibration of attention that happens when one's sustained exposure to a person whose attention is consistently organized differently begins to reshape one's own sense of what is worth noticing and who is worth stopping for. This is the formation Luke describes, and it does not happen through a program. It happens through the sustained, unmanaged, repeatedly disorienting experience of following someone whose sense of what matters is genuinely different from the one the surrounding culture has produced.

The Holy Spirit and the Formation of the Reader

Luke's sustained attention to the Holy Spirit carries a specific formative implication for the reader who engages the Gospel seriously over time: the same Spirit who fills Elizabeth and Mary and Zechariah and Simeon and Anna, who descends on Jesus at the baptism and leads him into the wilderness and empowers the Galilean ministry, is promised to those who ask. The promise is stated with unusual directness in the teaching on prayer: if you then, though you are evil, know how to give good gifts to your children, how much more will your Father in heaven give the Holy Spirit to those who ask him. The Spirit is not a theological category applied to exceptional moments of religious intensity. It is the active gift of a Father who is more eager to give than the asking community is to receive.

The formative implication of this for sustained engagement with Luke is the gradual recognition that the reading of the Gospel itself is a Spirit-attended activity — that the burning hearts of the Emmaus disciples as the Scriptures were opened to them describe not a unique first-century experience but the characteristic form of what happens when the text is engaged honestly and the Spirit attends the engagement. This is not a claim about emotional experience. It is a claim about the nature of the encounter the text makes possible: not the acquisition of historical information or the mastery of theological categories but the kind of knowing that reorganizes the reader from the inside, that leaves them asking afterward whether their heart was not burning, that produces in them something they did not bring to the reading and could not have generated without it.

Joy and the Formation of the Reader

The note of joy that Luke sounds from the first chapter through the last carries a specific formative function for the reader who returns to the Gospel across different seasons of life. In seasons of genuine difficulty — when the circumstances of daily life press against the goodness of what one believes and when the gap between the kingdom's announced presence and experienced reality is most acute — Luke's joy is not a comfort that minimizes the difficulty. It is the insistence that the difficulty is not the final word, pressed from multiple angles across the entire Gospel so that the reader who has been formed by sustained engagement with it has resources for the difficult seasons that the seasons themselves cannot generate.

The father who runs toward the returning prodigal is a resource for the season in which one is the prodigal — when the distance between where one is and where one should be feels too large to cross and the speech one has prepared feels inadequate to the reception one would need. The shepherd who leaves the ninety-nine is a resource for the season in which one feels lost — when the familiar markers of belonging and direction are not visible and the landscape of one's life does not correspond to the map one has been given. The woman who searches the house with a lamp is a resource for the season in which something essential has been lost and the search feels both necessary and uncertain. Luke's joy is not the joy of circumstances that have resolved themselves favorably. It is the joy of a God who searches and finds and runs and celebrates, available to people in every circumstance as the ground of a response that the circumstances themselves cannot produce.

Authority and the Formation of Community

Luke's sustained redefinition of authority — the authority that expresses itself through service rather than domination, through movement toward the last place rather than competition for the first, through the willingness to eat with the wrong people rather than the management of social association for strategic advantage — carries direct implications for how communities of faith form their own internal culture over time. The defining passage in chapter twenty-two, where Jesus responds to the disciples' argument about greatness at the Last Supper with the contrast between Gentile rulers and the one who serves, is addressed to a community that has spent the entire travel narrative being taught the same lesson from different angles and still needs to hear it again at the table the night before the cross.

The formation that sustained engagement with Luke's redefinition of authority produces is not the substitution of a service ethic for a dominance ethic within the same competitive framework. It is the gradual reorganization of the framework itself — the slow replacement of the question who is greatest with the question who is serving, and the further reorganization that produces when the community discovers that the answer to the second question consistently points toward people whose service was invisible within the framework the first question organized. Every community of faith faces the structural tendency to reproduce the Gentile model of authority within its own internal life, rewarding visibility and acknowledging influence while the people whose service is most consistent and most costly remain unrecognized by the metrics the community applies to significance. Luke's formation works against this tendency by repeatedly drawing attention to the wrong people in the position of exemplar, until the reader's sense of where to look for the kingdom's most significant action has been genuinely reorganized.

The Emmaus Pattern as the Shape of Sustained Reading

The Emmaus narrative in chapter twenty-four is the most complete portrait of what sustained engagement with Luke's Gospel is designed to produce. Two disciples who have lost their bearings — whose expectations have been shattered by the passion and whose hope has not yet been reorganized by the resurrection — walk toward Emmaus in conversation with a stranger who opens the Scriptures to them along the way. Their hearts burn within them. They recognize him in the breaking of the bread. They return immediately to Jerusalem. The sequence is the pattern: the disorientation that honest engagement with the cross produces, the opening of the Scriptures that reorganizes the framework for understanding what has happened, the recognition that comes not through argument but through a familiar gesture of reception, and the return to community and proclamation that the recognition generates.

The reader who returns to Luke repeatedly across different seasons of life will find that the Emmaus pattern recurs in each return: a season of disorientation or loss brings a new encounter with the text, and the text opens something in the new season that it could not have opened in the previous one, because the experience brought to the reading has given the text new purchase on a life that is now different from the life that read it before. The burning hearts of the Emmaus disciples are the experience of a text genuinely read and genuinely received — not mastered or completed but encountered afresh in circumstances that the previous reading could not have anticipated. This is what Luke does to the reader over time. It makes the one who walks beside them on the road increasingly recognizable, until the recognition that comes in the breaking of the bread is not the surprise it was the first time but the confirmation of what the burning heart has been registering all along.

Forgiveness and the Restoration of Those Who Have Failed

Luke's treatment of forgiveness across the entire Gospel — from the sinful woman's tears in the Pharisee's house through the criminal's request on the cross through Jesus' prayer for those who are crucifying him — constitutes one of the most pastorally significant contributions the Gospel makes to communities of faith in every generation. The formative dimension of this pattern for sustained reading is its gradual reshaping of the reader's own relationship to failure, to the failure of others, and to the kind of reception that genuine forgiveness requires the forgiven person to practice rather than simply believe.

The specific challenge Luke's treatment of forgiveness poses to the reader who engages it seriously over time is not primarily the challenge of extending forgiveness to those who have wronged them, though it includes that. It is the challenge of receiving forgiveness in the form Luke describes it — running toward, not waiting for the speech to be complete, restoring before the performance that would justify the restoration has been demonstrated. The reader who has been formed by sustained engagement with the father's running finds that their own experience of failure is met differently than it was before that formation: not with the expectation that the restoration must be earned by subsequent faithfulness, but with the recognition that the Father is already running, that the robe and the ring are already being prepared, and that what is required is not a better speech but the willingness to keep walking in the direction of home and to receive what is coming toward them before they have finished arriving.

Chapter 9

Reflection Questions

"But seek his kingdom, and these things will be given to you as well."
— Luke 12:31

Five Themes from Luke's Gospel

Luke's Gospel is designed not to be received as information but engaged as a living invitation — to the lost, to the poor, to the excluded, and to every reader who brings honest attention to what the Gospel actually says rather than what they expected it to say. Its careful ordering, announced in the prologue, is not the ordering of a document that arranges its argument for easy consumption. It is the ordering of a writer who has investigated the tradition and knows that the certainty it offers only becomes available to the reader who is willing to follow the argument all the way to where it leads. The following questions are offered as entry points for that kind of sustained, honest, repeatedly renewed engagement — not questions with definitive answers but questions that grow more rather than less demanding as the reader grows and as the circumstances of their life change around them.

These questions are organized around Luke's most distinctive themes rather than around the Gospel's narrative sequence, because the themes are what Luke's ordered argument is designed to press and because they are the points at which the Gospel most consistently creates the productive discomfort that genuine formation requires. They are designed to be returned to across different seasons of life, with the expectation that what they yield will be different at fifty than at thirty, not because the text has changed but because the life brought to it has deepened and the specific ways the Gospel's claims press against that life have become more visible.

On the Holy Spirit and Prayer

Luke's Gospel presents a Jesus who prays before every major turning point in his ministry and who teaches his disciples to pray with a persistence and a specificity that no other Gospel matches. What does the pattern of Jesus' prayer life in Luke reveal about the relationship between the mission he carries and the source from which it is sustained? Where in your own life is the gap between the centrality of prayer in Luke's portrait of Jesus and the actual place prayer occupies in the organization of your daily existence most visible and most honest?

The parable of the persistent widow is addressed explicitly to the need to pray always and not give up. The persistence it commends is not the mechanical repetition of requests but the sustained, specific, unembarrassed pressing of the kingdom's claim on the one who is able to answer it, in circumstances that have not yet confirmed the answer. Where in your own experience of prayer is the persistent widow's posture most difficult to maintain — where does the gap between what you are asking for and what you are experiencing most consistently produce the resignation that the parable is designed to address? And what would it mean to bring to that gap the widow's quality of continued, specific engagement rather than the management of expectation that protects against further disappointment?

The teaching on prayer in Luke culminates in a promise: how much more will your Father in heaven give the Holy Spirit to those who ask. The Spirit in Luke is not a reward for exceptional spiritual achievement. It is the gift available to those who ask, promised by the same Father whose generosity the parables of chapter fifteen describe. Where in your own spiritual life do you most need what the Spirit provides — the capacity to recognize what you cannot see from where you currently stand, the joy that the circumstances of the present moment cannot generate on their own, the power to embody the mission's directional consistency in conditions that resist it? And are you asking?

On Wealth and the Poor

Luke's Gospel contains more teaching on wealth, poverty, and economic life than any other Gospel, and it presses its argument with a specificity and a directness that general principles of generosity cannot absorb. Before engaging the specific questions the Gospel raises about wealth, the foundational question must be faced honestly: do you read Luke's economic teaching as addressed to you specifically, in your specific financial situation, with your specific relationship to your specific possessions? Or do you read it as addressed to people significantly wealthier than you are, leaving your own financial life outside the scope of its demands? The answer to this question determines the framework within which all the more specific questions are asked.

The rich man who builds bigger barns is condemned not for the barns but for the conclusion he draws from their fullness: that his soul is now secured for many years. What is the contemporary equivalent of the bigger barn in your own financial life — the specific form in which you are most tempted to locate your security in what you have accumulated rather than in the one who both gives and asks? The question is not whether accumulation is wrong in principle. It is whether the specific pattern of your financial choices reveals an orientation toward the security that accumulation provides that is competing with the orientation toward the kingdom that the Gospel commends.

Zacchaeus climbs a tree to see Jesus and comes down to give half his possessions to the poor and restore fourfold what he has taken. The response is disproportionate to anything Jesus has explicitly required of him, and it is the response of someone whose encounter with Jesus has produced an interior reorganization visible in the specific, concrete reordering of his financial life. Where in your own engagement with the gospel has that kind of interior reorganization occurred, and where has it remained at the level of stated value without producing the observable change in financial practice that Zacchaeus' response represents? The question is not whether you are generous by the standards of your surrounding culture. It is whether the pattern of your financial life corresponds to the pattern of a life genuinely organized around the kingdom rather than around the security that wealth provides.

On Inclusion and the Excluded

Luke's Gospel is saturated with the movement of Jesus toward people whom the surrounding culture had placed outside the boundaries of full social and religious participation. Women, lepers, Samaritans, tax collectors, Gentiles, the poor — the list is long and the pattern is consistent. The question this pattern presses on the modern reader is not whether they affirm inclusion as a general principle but whether the observable pattern of their actual community life corresponds to the directional consistency of Jesus' ministry in Luke. Whose company do you most consistently seek? Whose voices carry weight in your community's decisions? Who feels at home in your community and who, despite stated welcome, experiences the subtle signals that tell them the welcome does not quite extend to them specifically?

The parable of the Good Samaritan is addressed to a Torah expert who asks who is my neighbor, having already answered the great commandment's call to love the neighbor correctly. The follow-up question reveals the real concern: defining the boundary of the obligation so that its most demanding implications can be identified and, if necessary, excluded. Where in your own engagement with the command to love the neighbor are you most consistently pressing the same follow-up question — identifying the category of person whose claim on your attention the command does not quite reach, whose need is real but whose address requires crossing a boundary that your formation has told you is appropriate to maintain?

The elder brother stands outside the feast because he cannot bring himself to enter on the terms the feast requires. Those terms are not hidden: the father has explained them clearly. They require celebrating the return of someone whose departure the elder brother experienced as a betrayal and whose reception costs the elder brother something he would rather not give. Where in your own community life is there a person or a group whose full inclusion would reorganize the community in ways that you are not sure you are willing to accept — whose presence at the table would change the character of the table in ways that make you more sympathetic to the elder brother than you would like to be? The question is not whether the discomfort is real. It is whether you are willing to enter the feast anyway.

On the Parables and Self-Examination

Luke's parables function most powerfully not as illustrations of general truths but as mirrors in which the reader encounters their own position within the story they tell. The parable of the sower appears in Luke as it does in the other Synoptics, but Luke's version adds a detail that sharpens the self-examination it calls for: the seed that falls among thorns is choked by life's worries, riches, and pleasures. These are not extraordinary obstacles. They are the ordinary texture of daily life for people who are not in acute crisis — people who have enough, who are reasonably comfortable, and whose engagement with the gospel is genuine but whose soil condition is being determined by the accumulation of ordinary concerns rather than by any dramatic departure from faithfulness.

Which of the four soils most honestly describes the current condition of your own reception of the gospel? Not which you would most like to be, but which most accurately corresponds to what is actually happening to the word in your specific life right now.

The parable of the two sons in chapter fifteen — the prodigal and the elder brother — invites the kind of honest self-examination that only sustained engagement with both characters can produce. Most readers begin by identifying with the younger son, and that identification is genuine and important. But over time, and with the honesty that the elder brother's position requires, many readers discover that they have more in common with the one standing outside than with the one being feasted inside. Where have you stood outside a generosity you could not quite celebrate? Where has the good news of someone else's restoration produced in you something closer to the elder brother's resentment than to the father's joy? And what would it mean to acknowledge that honestly, and to take the father's invitation — son, everything I have is yours, come in — seriously enough to actually enter?

The parable of the Pharisee and the tax collector in chapter eighteen is the most direct mirror Luke offers for the reader's own prayer life. The Pharisee's prayer is not dishonest. He has done what he says he has done. The problem is not hypocrisy but the use of a genuine spiritual record as the ground of an approach to God that has no room in it for the tax collector's posture: God, have mercy on me, a sinner. Where in your own prayer life do you most consistently approach God with the Pharisee's résumé rather than the tax collector's honest need? And what would it mean to lay down the résumé — not to deny the faithfulness that has been genuine, but to recognize that the ground of approach the Gospel commends is the tax collector's posture rather than the Pharisee's record?

On Repentance and Restoration

The three parables of chapter fifteen press the same claim from three angles: something lost is found, and the recovery is celebrated with a joy that exceeds what observers think the occasion warrants. The chapter is addressed to Pharisees and scribes who are grumbling about Jesus' welcome of tax collectors and sinners, and the parables are designed to reorganize their sense of what constitutes an occasion for celebration. Where in your own experience of the gospel have you received a restoration that felt disproportionate to what you had earned — a reception more generous than you had prepared yourself for, a welcome that arrived before your speech of self-justification was complete? What did receiving that restoration rather than earning it actually require of you in terms of honest acknowledgment of your need and genuine receptivity to what was offered?

The father's running toward the prodigal is the Gospel's most concentrated image of the character of God's response to repentance. The running precedes the speech. The embrace precedes the explanation. The robe and the ring and the feast are organized before the prodigal has finished walking into the yard. Where in your own experience of failure and return has the restoration arrived faster than you expected, more generous than you deserved, and more specific than you had the confidence to ask for? And where has the experience of restoration been complicated by the sense that you needed to demonstrate sufficient remorse or subsequent faithfulness before you were fully entitled to receive what was already being offered?

Luke's Jesus prays from the cross: Father, forgive them, for they do not know what they are doing. The forgiveness is extended before the ones being forgiven have recognized their need for it, before they have repented, before they have done anything that would qualify them for the reception of what is being offered. This is the furthest reach of the pattern that runs through every parable of the lost — the forgiveness that moves toward the one who needs it before the one who needs it has begun moving toward the forgiveness. Where in your own life is there a person toward whom you are being called to move in this way — to extend the kind of forgiveness that does not wait for demonstrated remorse but that initiates the movement toward reconciliation from your side rather than waiting for the conditions to be established from theirs?

On the Travel Narrative and the Long Middle

The travel narrative of chapters nine through nineteen is Luke's primary location for the teaching that the community needs in the extended present between the resurrection and the return. The journey's destination is known, the pace of arrival is not, and the community must organize its life faithfully in the middle without collapsing the distance to the end or retreating into the safety of the beginning. Where in your own experience of faith do you most feel the pressure of the long middle — the gap between the kingdom's announced presence and the conditions that confirm it, the distance between the destination the gospel promises and the circumstances of the present moment that press against that promise?

The parable of the friend at midnight is addressed to the community in the long middle: ask, seek, knock, and the heavenly Father will give the Holy Spirit to those who ask. The persistence the parable commends is not the persistence of increasing desperation but the persistence of a community that knows both what it needs and who is able to provide it, and that continues to press the request with the combination of honesty and confidence that genuine relationship makes possible. Where in your own prayer life is the persistence, the parable commends most difficult to maintain, and what is the specific form that the temptation to stop asking takes in your own experience?

The parable of the ten minas, unique to Luke, is addressed to a community that expected the kingdom's full arrival to be immediate and that needed instruction about faithful stewardship in the extended period of the master's absence. The servant who buries his mina and returns it unchanged is not commended for prudence. He is condemned for the misunderstanding of the master's character that the burial reveals: I was afraid of you. Where in your own discipleship is the fear that produces the burying of what you have been given most operative — the sense that the risks of genuine engagement with the mission outweigh the risks of careful preservation of what you have received? And what does the master's response to the buried mina reveal about the character of the God whose absence the servant misread as a reason for fearful caution?

On the Table and Community

Luke records more meals than any other Gospel, and its sustained attention to who eats with whom carries direct implications for the actual table practices of communities of faith in every era. Before engaging the specific questions the table narratives raise, the foundational question must be asked honestly: in your community's common life, who actually eats with whom? Not who is theoretically welcome at every table, but who actually shows up at whose table for actual meals, in whose homes, under whose hospitality, with what regularity? The answer to this question is a more accurate description of your community's actual practice of inclusion than any stated commitment to welcome can provide.

The great banquet parable ends with a host who instructs his servant to go out and compel people to come in, because there is still room and the house is meant to be full. The compulsion is not coercion but the insistence of a generosity that will not be satisfied with a partial filling of the seats by people who present themselves without being sought. Where in your community's life is there the equivalent of the roads and country lanes — the places where people who would never present themselves at the door of the community are present and available to the invitation that is being extended? And what would the compel them to come in of the parable require of your community in terms of active, specific, personally extended invitation rather than the passive maintenance of a stated openness?

On the Cross and the Emmaus Pattern

The Emmaus narrative presents two disciples who have lost their bearings and a stranger who walks beside them, opens the Scriptures to them, and is recognized in the breaking of the bread. The disciples describe their experience afterward: were not our hearts burning within us while he talked with us on the road and opened the Scriptures to us? Have you had experiences of this quality — moments in which the engagement with Scripture produced something in you that you could not have generated yourself, a recognition that arrived not through argument but through an encounter whose character you recognized only after it had occurred? What were the circumstances that made that kind of encounter possible, and what has the experience of it revealed about the conditions under which the burning heart the Emmaus disciples describe becomes available?

The risen Jesus asks the Emmaus disciples whether it was not necessary that the Messiah should suffer these things and enter into his glory. The necessity is not fate but the internal logic of a mission whose character required the cross. Where in your own experience of following Jesus has the cross's necessity become most personally and most concretely real — where have the costs of the directional consistency the Gospel commends been most specific and most difficult, and what has the experience of those costs revealed about the relationship between the mission's character and the cost of maintaining it in conditions that resist it? And what has the continuation of the journey — the return from whatever form of Emmaus your own experience has taken — produced in terms of the recognition and the return that the Emmaus disciples' experience describes?

Questions for Continued Engagement

These questions are a beginning rather than an ending. Luke's Gospel is designed to generate more careful attention the more honestly it is engaged — not because it is obscure but because it is ordered, and the ordering reveals more of its argument the more completely the reader follows it. The reader who returns to Luke in six months or a year will find that the questions have not been answered and set aside but have deepened and shifted, not because the Gospel has changed but because the reader has, and because new circumstances have made different dimensions of the Gospel's argument newly immediate and newly demanding.

The most important thing about these questions is not that they be answered definitively but that they be taken seriously with the same quality of engagement that Luke's prologue models: the honest investigation, the careful ordering, the willingness to follow the argument where it leads rather than managing it at the level of familiarity with individual passages. The person who asks honestly, who does not settle for the comfort of the sentimental reading when the demanding one is what the text actually offers, who continues to bring the questions back to the text and to the community and to the experience of life lived in light of what the text claims, is practicing the kind of engagement that produces the certainty Luke promises Theophilus. Not the certainty of resolved questions but the certainty of a person who has followed the carefully ordered account all the way to where it leads and has found, in the breaking of the bread and the burning of the heart and the joy that the finding of the lost consistently produces, the confirmation that what Luke has investigated and written down is worth organizing a life around.

Chapter 10

Five Lessons

"For the Son of Man came to seek and to save the lost."
— Luke 19:10

Five Lessons from Luke's Gospel

The capacity of Luke's Gospel to shape communities of faith has not diminished across nearly two thousand years of engagement. The carefully ordered account that the prologue announces has proven capable of addressing communities as different from one another as the Gentile households of the first-century Mediterranean, the monastic communities of medieval Europe, the base communities of twentieth-century Latin America, and the diverse and fragmented communities of faith navigating the contemporary world. The reason is not that the Gospel is vague enough to mean anything to anyone. It is that the specific claims it makes about the character of the God who acts in Jesus, the scope of the people toward whom that action is directed, and the shape of the life that genuine reception of the gospel produces are claims that address dimensions of human experience that do not change with the century or the culture.

The five lessons that follow are not a summary of Luke's content. They are a distillation of the most persistent and most demanding things the Gospel asks of those who receive it — the things that remain pressing after all the historical context has been provided, all the structural features have been explained, all the theological categories have been identified. They are the lessons that remain when the reader has finished absorbing the information the Gospel provides and is left with the question the information has been building toward: what do you do with this? Each lesson is an answer to that question from a different angle, and together they constitute the response that Luke has been pressing its readers toward from the prologue's announcement of certainty to the final scene of great joy in the Temple.

Lesson One: The Gospel Moves Toward Those Who Have Been Left Out

Luke's most consistent and most theologically grounded lesson is the one that runs through the entire narrative from the shepherds in the fields to the criminal on the cross: the gospel moves toward those who have been left out. Not as a secondary application of principles established at the center, not as the extension of a welcome that is primarily organized around those who already belong, but as the primary and constitutive direction of the mission itself. The good news to the poor is not good news about something else that happens also to benefit the poor. The good news is the movement toward them, the stopping for them, the eating with them, the telling of stories in which they occupy the position of exemplar. The direction of the movement is the content of the announcement.

This lesson is stated most programmatically in the Nazareth synagogue, where Jesus reads from Isaiah and announces that the Spirit of the Lord is upon him because he has been anointed to proclaim good news to the poor. It is demonstrated most consistently in the pattern of encounters that follows: the leper who asks to be cleansed, the centurion whose servant Jesus heals across a social boundary that the centurion himself acknowledges he has no standing to cross, the widow of Nain whose son Jesus raises without being asked, the sinful woman who enters the Pharisee's house and is forgiven before she has made an articulate request, the Samaritan leper who alone returns to give thanks, Zacchaeus in his tree, the criminal on his cross. Each encounter is a fresh instance of the same directional movement, and the cumulative pattern is the argument: the gospel moves toward those who have been left out, and the community that carries the gospel carries the responsibility for continuing the movement.

The practical implications of this lesson for communities of faith in the contemporary world are extensive and resistant to the kind of general acknowledgment that leaves the actual practice of community life unchanged. Every community of faith organizes its attention and its resources around some people more than others, makes some people feel immediately at home and leaves others uncertain whether the welcome announced from the front extends to them in practice. The lesson Luke presses is not that every community should feel guilty about its current practice but that every community should examine honestly whether the directional movement of its actual life — the direction in which its attention, its resources, its most significant relationships, and its institutional energy consistently move — corresponds to the directional movement of the Gospel it proclaims. The community that has genuinely received this lesson will be recognizable not primarily by its stated values but by the observable pattern of where it consistently goes and who it consistently stops for.

The lesson also carries a specific challenge for individual readers. The movement toward those who have been left out costs something that is real and specific in every context where it is practiced: social capital, professional positioning, the management of reputation within communities that organize their approval around different values. The priest and the Levite who pass by on the other side of the road in the Good Samaritan are not heartless people. They are people whose formation has given them reasons for the direction they take, and those reasons are not irrational within the framework that produced them. The Samaritan's stopping is costly in ways the parable does not minimize: he uses his own oil and wine, puts the man on his own animal, takes him to an inn, pays the innkeeper, and promises to cover any further expense on his return. The movement toward those who have been left out in Luke is never a costless gesture of general goodwill. It is a specific, practically expensive, socially legible choice to go in the direction the gospel moves rather than the direction the surrounding culture commends.

Lesson Two: Prayer Is the Spine of the Mission

Luke's second lesson is the one its portrait of Jesus at prayer most insistently presses: prayer is not a supplementary spiritual practice for the devout but the spine of the mission, the sustaining relationship within which the entire enterprise of the gospel is conducted and from which it draws the resources that the mission itself cannot generate. Jesus prays at his baptism, before choosing the twelve, at the transfiguration, in Gethsemane, from the cross. The placement of prayer at every major turning point in the narrative is not biographical detail. It is a sustained theological claim about the nature of the mission: it is received and sustained in relationship with the Father rather than generated and maintained by the capacity of the one who carries it.

The teaching on prayer that the travel narrative concentrates is addressed to a community that needs this lesson not as inspiration but as instruction. The friend at midnight knocks at an hour when knocking is inconvenient and keeps knocking until the door is opened — not because the one inside is generous but because the one outside is persistent. The lesson is not that God is reluctant and persistence eventually wears him down. The lesson is that the posture of persistent, specific, continued pressing of the claim on the one who is able to answer it is the posture the community must maintain through circumstances that do not always confirm the responsiveness they are pressing toward. The persistent widow secures justice from an unjust judge by the same persistence. The comparison Jesus draws is from the lesser to the greater: if persistence secures justice from an unjust judge, how much more will the Father who loves those who cry out to him respond to those who keep asking?

For the community navigating the long middle between resurrection and return, prayer in Luke is the practice that sustains faithfulness through the gap between the kingdom's announced presence and the conditions of daily life that do not always confirm it. It is not the expression of a relationship that is going well. It is the practice that keeps the relationship alive through seasons when the gap between what is believed and what is experienced is most acute — the honest, specific, continued pressing of the claim on a Father whose character the parable of the running father has already revealed and whose responsiveness does not depend on the confirmation of visible circumstances. The community that prays as Luke commends is the community that has organized its life around the character of the one it is addressing rather than around the responsiveness of the circumstances surrounding the address. This is a genuinely difficult posture to maintain, and Luke's sustained teaching on prayer is his acknowledgment that it requires sustained instruction and the repeated renewal that comes from returning to the practice rather than from having mastered it.

The formative dimension of this lesson over time is the gradual replacement of prayer as religious obligation with prayer as the natural expression of a relationship that the mission requires. The disciples who ask Jesus to teach them to pray are not asking for a technique. They are asking to be shown what Jesus himself is doing when he withdraws to lonely places and prays before every significant decision and every significant act. The answer he gives them is not a formula to be recited but a pattern to be inhabited: an address that locates the one praying in relation to the Father, a request for the kingdom's coming and the daily provision it requires, an honest acknowledgment of the forgiveness needed and the forgiveness that must be extended, a petition for deliverance from the testing that the mission regularly produces. This is the spine of the mission, available to every community that is willing to inhabit it honestly rather than perform it decoratively.

Lesson Three: Joy Is the Accurate Response to What God Is Doing

Luke's third lesson is the one that the three parables of chapter fifteen press most completely and that the Gospel sustains from the first chapter's songs to the final chapter's great joy: joy is not a mood that favorable circumstances produce but the accurate response to what God is doing, available to those who have genuinely understood what that is regardless of the circumstances that surround the understanding. The shepherd's joy at finding the lost sheep is not produced by the improvement of his circumstances. The sheep's recovery is genuinely good, and the joy is the accurate response to a genuine good rather than the emotional product of a situation that has resolved itself favorably. The father's joy at the prodigal's return is not diminished by the elder brother's refusal to enter the feast. The son who was dead is alive, and the celebration is the accurate response to that reality whether or not everyone present is capable of sharing it.

This lesson has specific and demanding implications for communities of faith navigating circumstances that do not always confirm the goodness of what they believe. The joy Luke commends is not the performed positivity of communities that have decided to present their faith as attractive by suppressing honest engagement with what is genuinely difficult. It is the joy of the Emmaus disciples who have walked through the darkness of the passion and whose hearts are burning within them as the Scripture is opened — a joy that is available within the darkness rather than on the other side of it, grounded in the character of the one who walks beside them rather than in the resolution of the circumstances that make the walking difficult. This is joy as a form of knowledge rather than joy as an emotional state, available to people in circumstances that would not produce it by any other means.

The practical implication of this lesson is that communities of faith are called to embody a quality of joy that is recognizably different from the emotional postures the surrounding culture produces in people whose circumstances are comfortable, and that is also recognizably different from the emotional management of people who have been taught to perform contentment. Luke's joy is the joy of the woman who calls her neighbors to celebrate finding her coin — a joy that exceeds what observers think the occasion warrants because the observers are calculating the significance of the occasion by different standards than the woman is using. The community that has received this lesson will be recognizable by a quality of celebration that is disproportionate by the surrounding culture's standards and that the surrounding culture finds both attractive and puzzling, because it is being generated by something the surrounding culture has not provided and cannot replicate.

Lesson Four: The Kingdom Reorganizes Every Social Boundary

Luke's fourth lesson is the one that the Good Samaritan, the great banquet, the meal with Zacchaeus, the healing of the ten lepers, and the women who travel with Jesus all press from different angles: the kingdom's arrival reorganizes every social boundary that human communities have used to determine who belongs with whom, who has standing before God, and who is eligible for the good news the gospel announces. This is not a general principle of divine acceptance that dissolves all distinctions. It is the specific, culturally embedded, socially costly crossing of specific boundaries by the one who announces the kingdom's arrival, producing in its wake a community whose social arrangements can no longer be organized entirely around the logic of the boundaries that the surrounding culture maintains.

The lesson is pressed most directly in the parable of the great banquet, where the host's instruction — go out quickly into the streets and alleys of the town and bring in the poor, the crippled, the blind, and the lame — is followed by the discovery that there is still room, which produces the further instruction to go out to the roads and country lanes and compel them to come in, so that the house will be full. The boundary crossings are sequential and expanding: from the originally invited guests to the margins of the town, and then from the margins of the town to the people outside it entirely. The host's intention is a full house, and the fullness requires going further and crossing more boundaries at each stage until the house is actually full rather than merely open. This is the shape of the mission Luke describes, and the community that has received this lesson will find that the boundaries it must cross to maintain the mission's directional consistency keep extending further than the previous crossing prepared it for.

The practical implications of this lesson for the specific social arrangements of communities of faith in the contemporary world are both extensive and resistant to comfortable implementation. Every community of faith inherits from the surrounding culture a set of social arrangements that determine who naturally belongs together, whose presence is assumed and whose requires explicit effort, whose voices carry weight in the community's internal life and whose are heard as marginal or exceptional. The lesson Luke presses is not that these arrangements are the product of malice but that they are the product of formation, and that the formation the gospel commends moves consistently in a direction that the inherited arrangements consistently resist. The community that has genuinely received this lesson will be in a state of permanent gentle disruption of its own inherited social logic, not because disruption is a value in itself but because the directional consistency of the mission requires it and the character of the one who hosts the feast demands it.

The women in Luke's narrative are the most sustained instance of this lesson. Their presence at every significant moment of the narrative — the annunciation, the ministry, the cross, the tomb, the upper room — is not incidental background. It is the specific, repeated, socially legible crossing of the boundary that organized the surrounding culture's religious and public life most completely. The community that has received this lesson will find it pressing on the specific arrangements of its own common life: whose ministry is recognized and whose is invisible, whose leadership is assumed and whose requires explicit justification, whose presence at the most theologically significant moments of the community's life is natural and whose is exceptional. Luke's answer is that the women were there from the beginning, and the community that takes Luke seriously will find them there still.

Lesson Five: The Resurrection Transforms the Long Middle

Luke's fifth and final lesson is the one the Emmaus narrative states most completely: the resurrection does not end the long middle between the kingdom's arrival and its full completion, but it transforms it. The two disciples walking toward Emmaus are walking away from Jerusalem in the long middle — their hopes extinguished, their framework for understanding what has happened shattered, the period of waiting they are now inhabiting stripped of the expectation that had organized it. The resurrection does not immediately resolve their disorientation. It enters the disorientation alongside them, opens the Scriptures within it, and is recognized in the breaking of the bread at the end of the walk. The transformation is not the elimination of the long middle but the presence of the risen Jesus within it, making the walking different without making it unnecessary.

This lesson is Luke's most direct contribution to communities of faith navigating the specific challenges of the contemporary moment. The long middle is the permanent condition of the church between the ascension and the return, and the challenges it presents — the gap between the kingdom's announced presence and the conditions of daily life, the temptation to organize community life around institutional survival rather than missional direction, the erosion of the frameworks that have sustained faith across previous generations, the difficulty of maintaining the directional consistency of the mission in circumstances that reward different directions — are not exceptional challenges produced by the particular difficulty of the present moment. They are the characteristic challenges of the long middle in every generation, and Luke's Gospel was written for communities already inhabiting them.

The promise the resurrection carries in Luke is not the promise that the long middle will be shortened or that its challenges will be resolved by visible confirmation of the kingdom's presence. It is the promise of the Emmaus narrative: that the risen Jesus walks beside his community in the long middle, that the Scriptures opened along the way produce burning hearts even in the seasons when the destination feels uncertain, that the recognition that comes in the breaking of the bread is genuine and available to those who gather around it honestly. The community that has received this lesson will find that it organizes its life differently in the long middle than a community that has not — not with the anxious calculation of people who are trying to secure their institutional survival until the return, but with the quality of faithful engagement that the Emmaus disciples demonstrate when they return immediately to Jerusalem to tell what has happened on the road.

The urgency the resurrection generates in Luke is the urgency of commission rather than anxiety. The women leave the tomb and carry the news. The two disciples return from Emmaus to

Jerusalem. The disciples receive the commission to go to all nations beginning from Jerusalem and wait for the power from on high that will equip the going. The risen Jesus goes ahead, as he has always gone ahead, and the community that follows will find him in the places the commission sends it, recognizable in the familiar gesture of the one who takes bread and blesses it and breaks it and gives it. This is the transformation of the long middle that the resurrection produces: not the elimination of the waiting but the company of the one who walks beside those who wait, whose presence makes the burning hearts possible and whose recognition in the breaking makes the return to Jerusalem inevitable.

What Luke Has Given to the World

The influence of Luke's Gospel on the history of communities of faith is both extensive and distinctive. Its contribution is not primarily in the doctrinal formulations it has generated, though it has generated many. It is in the persistent, recurring pressure it has applied across every generation to the specific social arrangements that communities of faith inherit from the surrounding culture — the pressure toward the margins, the insistence on the table's open scope, the sustained attention to the women and the poor and the excluded that every generation must receive afresh because every generation inherits fresh versions of the arrangements that exclude them.

The conviction that the gospel's movement is consistently toward those who have been left out owes its most sustained narrative expression to Luke, which has supplied every movement in Christian history that has pressed communities of faith toward the margins with the specific, story-grounded, character-revealing portraits that make the pressure impossible to receive as a general principle without confronting its specific implications. The conviction that prayer is the spine rather than the supplement of the mission finds its fullest Gospel expression in Luke's portrait of Jesus at prayer before every turning point and in the concentrated teaching of the travel narrative. The conviction that joy is the accurate and disproportionate response to the gospel's arrival — that the celebration exceeds what observers calculate the occasion warrants because the observers are using different standards — is embedded in the three parables of chapter fifteen with a literary and theological craft that has not been surpassed in the history of religious literature.

This does not mean that communities formed under Luke's influence have been consistently faithful to its vision. Institutions that invoke the name of the one who came to seek and save the lost have organized themselves around the protection of those who are already found. Communities that read the Magnificat have maintained social arrangements that correspond to the order it announces is being overturned. Those who tell the story of the prodigal's father have stood in the elder brother's position outside feasts that a generosity they could not celebrate was organizing inside. Acknowledging this history is not a reason to abandon Luke. It is a reason to return to it with the honest, investigated, ordered engagement that the prologue commends, allowing the text to press its specific claims against the specific arrangements of each new generation with the same directness it has always pressed them.

The Enduring Questions

The questions that Luke's Gospel raises cannot be finally answered by any human arrangement and will therefore continue to press themselves on every community and every individual in every era. They are questions about the scope of the gospel's movement — whether the community's practice of welcome corresponds to the directional consistency of the mission or has been organized around the social logic of the surrounding culture.

110

They are questions about the economic implications of the kingdom's arrival — whether the actual financial life of the community and its members reflects the reorganization the gospel commends or has been managed at the level of principle while the specific arrangements of financial life remain largely unchanged. They are questions about who is at the table and what that reveals about the actual scope of the welcome the community practices.

These questions are currently being asked with unusual urgency in the contemporary world, because the communities that previously provided frameworks for belonging, for the management of failure, and for the orientation of life toward something more adequate than private accumulation have eroded significantly, and the hunger for something more adequate than what the surrounding culture offers is everywhere evident in forms that range from the explicitly religious to the inarticulate. Luke's response to this condition is the same response it has always offered: here is the one who came to seek and save the lost, who eats with sinners and crosses the boundaries that organize exclusion and tells stories in which the wrong people are in the position of exemplar and runs toward the returning prodigal before the speech has been completed. Come and see. Come and follow. Come and find that the table is larger than you expected and that there is room enough for the feast the host intends.

The Character of Sustained Reading

Reading Luke well over a lifetime requires the cultivation of habits of reading that do not develop without intention and repeated return to the text across different seasons of life. The most important is the habit the prologue models: the willingness to investigate honestly, to consult the sources carefully, to arrange the engagement with ordered intention, and to pursue the certainty that the things one has been taught are true rather than settling for the comfort of a familiarity that mistakes knowing the stories for having received their claim. Luke is designed to be read by people who want to know, in the fullest sense of that word — not merely to possess accurate information but to have their framework for understanding reorganized by an encounter with something more adequate than the framework they brought to it.

The reader who returns to Luke across different seasons of life will find that sustained engagement produces a specific kind of formation that cannot be achieved by any other means. Not the formation of comprehensive theological mastery but the formation of a person who has been shaped over time by sustained exposure to the portrait of the God who runs and searches and celebrates and walks beside people on the road to Emmaus and is recognized in the breaking of bread. This formation follows the same pattern as the formation of the disciples in the travel narrative: it does not require extraordinary preparation or exceptional capacity. It requires the willingness to keep showing up, to keep bringing one's actual experience honestly rather than the polished version, to keep allowing the text to press its specific claims toward the specific conditions of one's specific life rather than maintaining the comfortable distance of general appreciation.

The Permanent Invitation

The invitation that Luke extends across twenty-four chapters is the invitation that the Emmaus narrative describes most completely: come and walk, and let the Scripture be opened to you along the way, and stay for the breaking of the bread, and discover in the recognition that the walking and the opening and the breaking produce that the one who walked beside you was always the one Luke has been describing from the prologue's announcement to the Temple's great joy. It is an invitation addressed to people who do not fully understand what they are accepting, whose frameworks will be reorganized by the encounter in ways they did not anticipate, whose hearts will burn within them in moments they will not have predicted, and who will find themselves returning to Jerusalem — returning to the community and the proclamation and the practice of the mission — because the recognition has made the return both inevitable and joyful.

Luke was not written to produce people who have understood the gospel completely and are living it out with consistent adequacy. It was written for Theophilus and for everyone like him — people who have received the gospel from outside their own tradition, who need the certainty that comes from careful investigation rather than inherited familiarity, who are navigating the long middle between the kingdom's arrival and its full completion in communities that do not always correspond to the scope of what they have been taught, and who need the specific, ordered, eyewitness-grounded account of what the one who came to seek and save the lost actually did and said and was. For readers who bring to Luke the honest and sustained engagement it deserves, the most important thing the Gospel contains is not the sophistication of its literary arrangement or the specificity of its historical grounding, but the portrait of the God who runs — who is always already running, toward the prodigal while he is still a long way off, toward the lost sheep on his shoulders, toward Emmaus alongside the people who have stopped expecting him — and whose running is the ground of the joy that Luke has been pressing its readers toward from the first chapter's songs to the last chapter's great joy in the Temple.

Closing Reflection

*"Were not our hearts burning within us while he talked with us on
the road and opened the Scriptures to us?"*
— Luke 24:32

Luke's Gospel has endured because the scope it carries does not
shrink. Who is my neighbor? What does good news to the poor
actually mean when it is received by people who are not poor?
What kind of community does the kingdom of God call into
being, and by what pattern of running toward and eating with and
telling stories about the wrong people is that community sustained
across the centuries and the cultures and the specific social
arrangements of each generation's particular moment? These are
not questions that belong to the first century alone. They are
questions that each generation must face with the honesty and the
specificity they deserve, and Luke is designed to make that honest
engagement both possible and unavoidable for those who bring
sufficient attention to it.

What gives Luke its lasting power is not the beauty of its
narratives alone, though those narratives — the Good Samaritan,
the Prodigal Son, the road to Emmaus — have shaped the moral
imagination of communities of faith and of the wider culture more
durably than almost any other stories in the history of religious
literature. It is the claim at the center of every one of them: that in
the person of Jesus of Nazareth, the God of Israel acted to seek
and save the lost, that the scope of who is lost is wider than any
community has yet been willing to acknowledge, and that the joy
produced by each finding is disproportionate to what observers
calculate the occasion warrants because the observers are using
the wrong standard. This claim is either true, or it is not, and Luke
does not allow its readers to hold it at a comfortable distance
where it can be appreciated as literature without being engaged as

gospel. The father runs. The question is whether the reader will receive what he is running toward them to give.

One of the most characteristic features of Luke's Gospel, observed across the entire history of its reception by communities of faith in every era and every cultural context, is its resistance to being received as inspiration without being received as demand. The parable of the Good Samaritan ends with a command: go and do likewise. The Beatitudes come with corresponding woes. The great banquet's host instructs the servant to go out and compel people to come in until the house is full — not to announce that the house is open and wait for people to discover the invitation. The Magnificat announces reversals that the Gospel then demonstrates are not merely eschatological promises but descriptions of what the kingdom's arrival produces in the specific social and economic arrangements of communities that genuinely receive it. Luke is the Gospel that most consistently refuses to let the beauty of the story insulate the reader from the demand the story is making.

Luke was written by someone who took the craft of writing seriously enough to say so before beginning, who investigated everything from the beginning and consulted the eyewitnesses and arranged the account with ordered intention. That investment in the craft of ordered account is not ornamental. It is the formal expression of the conviction that the things Theophilus has been taught are true in the way that investigated, eyewitness-grounded, carefully ordered accounts of historical events are true — not merely true in the sense that they are spiritually meaningful or morally instructive but true in the sense that they correspond to what actually happened, and that what actually happened is the most significant sequence of events in human history. The certainty Luke's prologue promises is the certainty of a claim that has been investigated and found to bear the weight of investigation. It is available to every reader who is willing to bring the same quality of honest engagement to the reading that Luke brought to the writing.

Reading Luke well over a lifetime produces a specific and irreplaceable formation. Not the mastery of its historical context or the completion of its theological categories, but the gradual reshaping of the reader's sense of who is worth stopping for, what constitutes genuine celebration, what prayer looks like when it is honest rather than performed, and where the kingdom's activity is most concentrated in the specific landscape of one's daily life. The reader who returns to Luke in different seasons will find that the parables yield something new in each return — that the elder brother's position outside the feast looks different from inside one's own version of faithfulness than it did from the outside, that the persistent widow's continued pressing of her claim looks different in a season of genuine unanswered prayer than it did in a season of confirmation. The text meets the reader where they actually are, and the depth of the meeting is proportional to the honesty with which the reader brings their actual situation.

The Emmaus narrative is the image of what this sustained engagement produces over time. Two disciples who have lost their bearings walk alongside a stranger who opens the Scriptures to them, and their hearts burn within them without their knowing why. They recognize him in the breaking of the bread and return immediately to Jerusalem. This is the pattern of sustained reading: the disorientation that honest encounter with the cross produces, the opening of the Scripture that reorganizes the framework for understanding what has happened, the recognition in a familiar gesture of reception, and the return to community and proclamation that the recognition makes inevitable. The reader who has engaged Luke seriously across years will find this pattern recurring in each engagement — the burning hearts that precede the recognition, the recognition that sends them back, the going back that prepares the next encounter.

The invitation that Luke extends is the same invitation it has always extended, to Theophilus and to every reader since: come and know the certainty of the things you have been taught. Not the certainty of arguments that have never been pressed, not the certainty of a faith that has never been tested by the specific circumstances of a specific life, but the certainty that comes from sustained, honest, investigated engagement with the account of the one who came to seek and save the lost and who demonstrated across twenty-four chapters what seeking and saving looks like when it is conducted by someone who runs rather than waits, who eats with the wrong people rather than managing association for advantage, who tells stories in which the wrong characters are in the position of exemplar, and who is recognized in the breaking of the bread by people who had stopped expecting him to be present.

Luke's Gospel will keep pressing what it has always pressed as its readers keep bringing more to it. The questions it generates do not resolve into comfortable answers. The scope it announces does not shrink to a manageable size. The joy it commends does not diminish with familiarity. And the God it describes does not become less present to those who keep walking toward Emmaus in the honest acknowledgment of what they do not yet fully understand. The invitation the burning hearts extend is the same invitation the running father embodies: come as you are, as far along or as far away as you currently are, and discover in the encounter that the one who is running toward you was always who Luke said he was — and that the life organized around his character is, as Luke has been insisting from the prologue's first word to the Temple's final joy, the only life worth the name.

The Bible for Modern Life Series

This book is part of **The Bible for Modern Life** series—an ongoing collection that explores the meaning, historical setting, and message of individual books of Scripture.

Each volume looks closely at the biblical text to help readers understand what it meant in its original context and how its truths still apply to life today.

The goal is simple: to help modern readers engage more deeply with the Bible—one book at a time.

— Samuel Whitaker